REVOLT, SHE SAID

This work, published as part of a program of aid for publication, received support from the French Ministry of Foreign Affairs and the Cultural Service of the French Embassy in the United States.

Philippe Petit's interview was originally published in French as *Contre la dépression nationale*, by Les Editions Textuel, Paris

Semiotext(e)
2571 W. Fifth Street
Los Angeles, CA 90057
www.semiotexte.org

501 Philosophy Hall
Columbia University
New York, NY 10027

Design: Hedi El Kholti
Cover picture: John Foley / Opale
Special thanks to Giancarlo Ambrosino

Distributed by The MIT Press, Cambridge, Mass. and London, England

ISBN: 1-58435-015-6
Printed in the United States of America

REVOLT, SHE SAID

JULIA KRISTEVA

An Interview by Philippe Petit

Translated by Brian O'Keeffe
Edited By Sylvère Lotringer

SEMIOTEXT(E) FOREIGN AGENTS SERIES

CONTENTS

FOREWORD

"Nobody died, so nothing happened." This comment by the philosopher Alexandre Kojève[1] sounds very much like a political judgment. But it is neither a moral condemnation of the events of 1968 nor an expression of contempt at the ambitions of the student movement; rather, it is a historical analysis of what, arguably, were the negative features of this revolt against General de Gaulle and the renewed prestige of France. Nobody died: the spoilt children of the bourgeoisie just aimed for the wrong target. For Kojève, the sage Hegelian, questioning the bourgeois state was neither a figure of conscience, nor was it a responsible action informed by the end of History and the advanced stage of the Gaullist state. It was an abortive revolt against Mother and Father France—a family psychodrama.

Was May '68 just a historical parody in bad taste? Kojève wasn't the only person to think so. Edgar Morin[2] spoke more indulgently of a "jamboree" and of "guerrilla play acting" in the sense that the events "allowed the barricades of French history and Che's guerrillas to be undermined." The May movement was only a parenthesis, a moment of insolence and contestation with neither a true historical perspective nor a serious program. Children played at revolution, the workers, employees and nurses had joined them, and the nationalist right ordered them all to get back in line.

May had started in the Latin Quarter and ended on the sacred way that leads from Place de la Concorde to the Arc de Triomphe. May had blossomed on the cobbles of the rue Gay-Lussac and had withered on the pavement of the Champs-Elysées. The rebels had risen up against a faceless power and the Gaullists had shown themselves in the company of "deportees in their camp stripes, veterans sporting their decorations, ex-Resistants wearing their old armbands." 1944-1968: it had come full circle, so parents could sleep easier and children could grow up in peace. "The rains of August seem to have dampened the fires of May to smoke and ash. In an emptied-out Paris, the streets and then the walls have been cleaned. This cleaning-up operation affected the mind too, where memories are wiped clean," wrote Michel de Certeau[3] in *La Prise de la parole (The Capture of Speech)* which appeared in October 1968.

The legend of May began, there were endless books on the events, the '68 intellectuals were getting ready for conversion. This legend, turned into a vulgate version, is too pessimistic. The democratic revolution of '68 was said to have been an impossible revolution, a revolt against authority, political parties, institutions, phallocentrism, etc.; it was said to have been a growing pain, a sterile face-off between the moral order and the disorder of desire, an absurd joust between rules and their opposite. How mistaken! How naïve! Except for the "new philosophers," there is no-one who actually thinks revolutions turn out for the better. All revolutions peter out, but that fact has never prevented people from rebelling. "The experience of rules," said Georges Canguilhem[4], "is the testing of the regulatory function of rules in irregular circumstances." It's not the refusal of rules. Revolt against the State isn't a negation of the policies of the State, just as dissent over family values is not a negation of Family. May '68 was first and foremost about rejecting statism, familialism, authoritarianism; it was about the promise of love without conjugality, the affirmation of unprecedented possibility; it was, according to Julia Kristeva, a furious search for happiness and a thirst for the sacred: "a violent desire to rake over the norms."

Thirty years after the May movement it seemed timely for us to draw out the consequences of this "liberation-revolt" and to ask the author of *Les Nouvelles Maladies de l'âme* (1993, texts from 1979, tr. *New Maladies of the Soul*) why "the questioning of laws, norms and values is the crucial moment in the psychic life of individuals, as it is for societies." A writer and psychoanalyst, born in 1941 in Bulgaria, Julia Kristeva came to France at Christmas, 1965, where she discovered a shaken France that had just come out of the Algerian war and was retracting to a proud but anxious Gaullism. A privileged witness of events, at the age of 27 and within *Tel Quel* magazine[5], she discovered the effervescence of the avant-gardes, she got close to the CGT trade union and the Communist Party, listened at the grass roots, admired the poet-president Mao. Over the years she rejected "hard-core" feminism, decrypted Jacques Lacan[6], worked with Roland Barthes[7] and Claude Lévi-Strauss[8], read Louis Althusser[9]. The foreigner made her way and cultivated her love for French literature and for Freud. Saturated with theory, she felt the need to look inward, and began psychoanalysis in 1973. She came out of it an analyst and novelist. Nobody died (although there were three activists who did, all the same), but very early on Julia

Kristeva grasped what was essential about the May 1968 events. She quickly understood that what was being expressed then was the need for social cooperation. Society, *pace* Kojève, isn't a closed totality. Individuals always have the opportunity to scrutinize norms. There is no absolute contradiction between the affirmation of desire and the imposition of a limit. But, on the other hand, one can't "touch base" with oneself without revolt.

"Happiness only exists at the price of revolt" declared the author of *Histoires d'amour* (1983, tr. *Tales of Love*). That goes for both intimate and social experience. That was the good news of May, the message communicated to the *enragés*[10]. The wish to join private pleasure and public happiness remains a new idea for each of us. The revolution of democracy and solidarity has only just begun.

Philippe Petit

WHAT'S LEFT OF 1968?

The Freedom to Revolt □ "We Want the Impossible" □ Exaltation of the Negative and the Moment of Rupture □ Sexual Liberation and Sexual Religion □ The Catastrophic and the Erotic □ *Anti-Oedipus* □ Law and Prohibition □ Resurgence of the Sacred □ Complex Paternity □ Brotherly Love and Homosexuality □ Death of God and the 1968 *Enragés* □ The Figure of the Mother □ Not a Theorist of Feminism—New Maladies of the Soul □ Happiness and the Sacred □ Hannah Arendt □ I Rebel, Therefore I Am

"Among the sixty-eighters who converted en masse *to realism, it has become fashionable to reduce May '68 to a cultural and sociological phenomenon. It's assumed to be about young people rising up against an outdated and highly centralizing State, against strict moralities and rigid hierarchies." This was Daniel Bensaïd's comment in a 1993 article for* Rouge *(Red) magazine[11]. What do you think of this judgment? Have we downgraded the events of 1968 to a counter-cultural rebellion? Thirty years later, aren't we discounting the general strike and the social movement that accompanied it?*

One word on everyone's lips in May '68 was "contestation." It expresses a fundamental version of freedom: not freedom to change or to succeed, but freedom to revolt, to call things into question. Thirty years on, because of technology and liberalism, we're so used to identifying freedom merely with free enterprise that this other version doesn't seem to exist; it's got to the point where the very notion of liberty is fading in people's minds and absent from their actions. Remember, liberty-as-revolt isn't just an available option, it's fundamental. Without it, neither the life of the mind nor life in society is possible. I mean "life" here, and not just maintenance, repetition, management. The telling moment in an individual's psychic life, as in the life of societies at large, is when you call into question laws, norms and values. You can't deplore the "death of values" and discount the movements that question them, as some are doing. Because it's precisely by putting things into question that "values" stop being frozen dividends and acquire a sense of mobility, polyvalence and life. There was no nihilism in the contestation that burned up that month of May 1968; instead it was a violent desire to rake over the norms that govern the private as well as the public, the intimate as well as the social, a desire to come up with new, perpetually contestable configurations. This desire for an exhilarating and joyful "permanent revolution" was perhaps just part and parcel of young people abreacting their "second Oedipus," i.e. their adolescence, on the back of an obsolete State and a prurient consumer society. But by all accounts, it was sexual and cultural contestation that spearheaded events, and young people were rightly mistrustful of the political "co-opting" the trade unions and left-wing parties tried to impose on that "spring," as well as the workers' intrinsic "consumerism." It's still true, though, that the general strike and the social movement that shook up the country can be interpreted, from a distance, as the symptom of something altogether new. On the one hand it was the desire of the most disadvantaged citizens—the "humiliated" and the "offended"—to claim a dignity beyond and actually in spite of the political structures that had usually served them since the industrial revolution. On the other, this also indicated the final stage of the "proletariat" in the sense of a homogenous class and a certain clientele of political parties. While the process of discrediting political frameworks was going on, the "humiliated" and "offended" became aware that they were subjects who shouldn't be relegated to their status as producers in the system of production. For while keeping up their legitimate claims to better salaries and working conditions, they were also carried away by the demands of subjective freedom. This led them to ask for greater democracy, less centralization and finally, greater happiness for all. And also the right to respect, besides the right to consume. What we describe as the "advances of democracy" of these last thirty years includes above all the self-assurance of the poorer classes, daring to claim the same pleasures—if not the same luxuries—as the others. It's a real '68 kind of claim: "We're realists, we want the impossible." Does the impossible mean happiness? The impossible and more— happiness for all.

We often forget that the impulse of the French Revolution of 1789 was a new idea, happiness for the greatest number of disadvantaged people. This wasn't like the American revolution, far more legalistic and federalist in spirit, which offered better management of the contract that rather well-off freeholders were making amongst themselves. Possibly because of my foreign origins, I'm more sensitive than most to the difference that exists between these two revolutions, and to the fact that in France there is a *people* which hasn't forgotten it carried out the most radical of the bourgeois revolutions. The most violent, certainly, and its consequences are still problematic, but the most grounded in the miserable reality that is still the lot of our continent. It was also linked to Christian and Rousseauistic ambitions of dignity for all. The youthful contestation of May 1968 wasn't blind to that tradition, and its rejection of the Communist or Socialist parties didn't make it any the less attentive to the social movement—on the contrary. You know as I do that many leftists who occupied the Odéon theatre went to "establish" themselves in a factory! We know about the misgivings of political leaders towards this "mayhem," from De Gaulle up to Mitterrand; they didn't want people to link the disruption of France in 1968 and the socialist victory in 1981. They all mistrusted permanent contestation and we can imagine only too well what good reasons they had. However, it was May 1968 that brought about this renewed questioning of overbearing hierarchies and the absolutes of productivist society, and it's very much by virtue of its impetus that France braced itself to begin the slow modernization still ongoing today. It's happening through the advances and failures of the socialists up to the ecology and the unemployed movements. This sort of modernization doesn't just yearn to adapt to the imperatives of globalization (while acknowledging them), but tries to tackle the postindustrial age with very "French" attributes such as taste and the art of living—though without any throw-backs to the idle country of the good old days. What is this right to extravagance, if not each individual, down to the humblest person, having an irreducible aspiration to dignity? And you'll forgive that word, because that's the way some perceive the French version of liberty, liberty May '68 style.

I think this dual aspect of the "spirit of '68"—at once freeing subjective desires and concern for the dignity of the most disadvantaged—is one of the features of the movement in France. It's more evident than in other countries, which have experienced the ardent flames of sexual liberation, but with less philosophical underpinning and less involvement from popular movements.

At the time, did you have the feeling of following up on a history that started in 1848, then 1870 and then in 1936? Was there the impression of living through one of these Parisian revolts that make up the history of the French Republic?

I came to France at Christmas, 1965; in May 1968 I had only known what France was like for two years. It was an extraordinary time to be learning about French culture and politics. All the more so since, unlike my French friends, I had no family in France to "contest" nor a "bourgeois tradition" to reject or improve. From the start, my view of events went beyond my personal history and its particular burdens; I looked at events from a long-term perspective, as a continuation of the spirit of the 1789 Revolution, the revolutionary movements that date back to 1848, of course, and even more so, the Paris Commune[12].

Were you reading the classics on 1848 and the Commune?

You didn't get to read much in May '68. The chaos and agitation overtook moments of reading, but in fact there were two or three texts lying around on my desk at that time. I quoted them a lot in the doctoral thesis I published later as *Révolution du langage poétique. L'avant-garde à la fin du XIXe siècle: Mallarmé et Lautréamont* (1974, tr. *The Revolution in Poetic Language*). First of all, there was Marx's *18th Brumaire*, which seemed to me to be a pitiless though just analysis of French society, which he described as a "sack of potatoes," i.e. a bunch of awkward individualisms—the ones May '68 rightly rose up against. Also, Marx had seen both the signs of revolutionary movements and their failures very clearly, starting with the Revolution. As far as I am concerned, this book is still up to date. I was also reading Hegel's *Logic*. What I got from his dialectic was above all the exaltation of the negative. The moments of rupture dazzled me; they seemed to resonate with what was going on in the streets, as well as with the psychic life specific to literary creation. I began to get interested in psychoanalysis, and the relationship between psychosis and modern art seemed self-evident to me: it weighs in on the side of the negative Hegel posits as immanent to the life of the mind, and which Freud was to rework in terms of the "rejection" of the drives and the "negativity" that are both internal to judgment. Today some philosophers and sociologists tend to discredit this valorization of the negative to the advantage of the "system," because it's that which seems to them more appropriate to the psychic and social realities of the present day. When it comes down to it, they let themselves get carried away by the desire to manage the *status quo*; they heavily underestimate the damage as much as the re-birth it can bring about. Finally, I remember a poem of Victor Hugo's that left its mark on me in my childhood and which I've since passed on to my son: it seemed to encapsulate France's daring and insolent youthfulness. It was in perfect consonance with those events—less the blood, fortunately: "On a barricade, among the paving stones/ Spattered with guilty blood and by purer blood washed away/ A child of twelve is captured with the men/ Are you with those lot? The child says: we're part of them." (*L'Année terrible,* June 1871, number 11.)

There are two daguerreotypes of the rue Saint-Maur barricade in 1848, taken before and after the riot, two photos taken by someone at a window...

I remember when we dug up the paving stones from the rue Gay-Lussac. We tried to build a barricade, which wasn't as impressive as the ones I imagined were in Hugo, but it was quite something, though! Then there was the charge by the police and we sheltered in the Ecole Normale; it was surrounded. We couldn't get out.

Sollers[13] pretended to be a doctor accompanying a stretcher-bearer; I got away in the chaos caused by the tear gas.

There was the rue Gay-Lussac and the Renault factory at Billancourt, the Latin Quarter and the Wonder factories. Did you ever want to "establish" yourself in a factory?

Not really. In Bulgaria, the Communist party put young people into factories or co-op farms to teach them about reality and to fight the intellectuals' elitism. Above all, it denigrated intellectual work. Intellectuals came out of it more humiliated than "realistic." What I got from this was a great respect for those who live by the mind, and I have it still. It's quite a rare activity, isn't it, and one that deserves to be encouraged, surely not converted into another function, even if it were to be productive in terms of consumer goods. All the more so since intellectuals don't have much to teach workers in the factory itself, it's simply by their books. My friends who established themselves in a factory in May 1968 afterwards seemed to me to have a lot of psychological difficulties, a great feeling of guilt and no self-confidence. I had just read Saint Thomas, who took up the Biblical and evangelical precept to love thyself as thy neighbor, and advised the believer to "Establish yourself within yourself!" It's a sublime phrase that in the end invites us to be reconciled to our narcissism before we establish links with anyone else. Any link with "vanity" (or what we call egotism) is unfailingly denounced. It's quite the opposite, because to "establish oneself within the self" guards against any excesses of egocentricity. So I used to say to one of my friends whose establishment in a factory ended in a lot of bitterness: "Establish yourself within yourself and you'll choose afterwards if you can get established elsewhere." He saw what I was saying, but only a few years later, after his painful experience.

At this distance, what would you say about the liberation of social behavior that all of the sixty-eighters took part in to a greater or lesser extent?

I have just said the word "experience": the liberation of social behavior was an essential experience of '68. Group sex, hashish, etc., were experienced as a revolt against bourgeois morality and family values. All of us from my generation went through it. This movement can only be described as political because it began by striking savagely at the heart of the traditional conception of love. A few years before, we had discovered sex shops. Many of us went to Holland first of all, to Scandinavia and the north to take advantage of the loosening up of restrictions. Then the wave hit France. It was new and *risqué* at the same time, so it was a drug...

I get the picture, but this revolution in behavior, this sexual revolution, this exhibition of bodies, this breach with what was considered a family and moral order, how do you see it today?

I think it's indispensable, because it's this liberated behavior that contributed to the liberation of French society, still straight-jacketed in old nineteenth-century ways, terrified by the Algerian war... You shouldn't forget that '68 was a worldwide movement that contributed to an unprecedented reordering of private life. My misgivings start with the commercialization of this breakthrough, when this great upheaval became an ideology of pleasure and the body, the marketing of sense-less entertainment. That always leads to anxiety. Today, sexual liberation has degenerated into "health sex": an idyllic panacea, a new religion that finishes up as a cocoon or as family life reinstated in a sort of oceanic feeling, where there's pleasure for all, at any price, no problems. As if there were equality in pleasure, as if Eros weren't the other face of Thanatos!

"Holistic" sex has transformed itself into universal peace, regulated by spectacle and profit, and has ended up confused with the death of desire...

Did you quickly become aware of this recuperation?

The liberation movement distrusted partisan recuperations, but didn't immediately suspect the media and the market-place of recuperating their desire by packaging it or turning it into images. Even though Guy Debord's distrust of the society of the spectacle[14] made itself felt very early on (in 1967), his indictment was only known to a small group. The slogan "recuperation—a trap for nerds" spread quickly, but essentially to attack political positions, or for intervening in university matters. We often had the impression that as soon as something new was on offer, it became an institution. As far as sex is concerned, most didn't have this impression. Perhaps they let themselves get trapped, particularly by psychedelia—sexual liberation with a hint of paradise—so that the heat of battle cooled and left only a hazy religion. Possibly they let themselves get carried away by that so very French, libertine ideology of salvation through desire, i.e. without desire, no salvation. Still, there were many "enterprises" to transform sexual liberation into a sexual religion. And this was the beginning of the end, it *established* what was facile about it all. A new kind of consensus! Although you often hear about sex-haters who pretend to be just against its abusive marketing, they're really just puritans! And because hypocrisy is difficult to flush out—except in the bedroom, though very few have the courage to surrender there!—I prefer to encourage those who are still making an attempt at liberation, especially a sexual one, than to follow the ones who are prosecuting the abuses of this freedom.

When did you get really interested in psychoanalysis? In 1968, you didn't yet know that you would become a psychoanalyst. What were the factors that made you make this choice?

First of all, thanks to seeds sown by French civilization. Beside the abyssal metaphysics of German philosophy, with Kant, Hegel and Heidegger, and English empiricism, from Locke to the logical-positivists, what's specific about French thought is that it's written with immediacy (following on from Descartes and Pascal and then Voltaire, Diderot and Rousseau), and it's also corporal, sexualized, i.e. thought and literature coming together with the same concern for sexual truth—Villon, Rabelais, the eighteenth century. In modernity, from Diderot and de Sade to Proust and Bataille, this way of taking into account sexual experience and its co-presence with thought is unique to France. Here we're at the source of what's called French atheism: a strange valorization of a very particular psychic life, inasmuch as it is sustained by sexual desire and rooted in bodily needs; it exhausts transcendence though in no way denies it, instead it brings such incarnate transcendence back into meaning. Next, the prominence sexuality had in May 1968 could only direct my attention once again to Freudianism, which was by no means something wholly abstract to me. The unconscious, dreams, drives: that was just how we were living, in the heat of the moment. Finally, there was the prestige of this revival of psychoanalysis that thinkers like Lévi-Strauss contributed to. He had introduced the problematics of incest into anthropology while still keeping his distance from Freud; Althusser used Freudian notions in his analysis of Marxism; Barthes hybridized structuralism by delving into the sexual secrets of the text. Above all, Lacan disrupted linguistics and phenomenology by contaminating Saussure's "signifier" and Heidegger's "Being" with insatiable desire and its lack, or his "object *little a.*"[15] What was most active and original in French cultural life from 1960 to 1970 was therefore impregnated with Freud's discoveries, and I just immersed myself in that when my turn came along.

Fine. But you could as easily have become a follower of Deleuze[16]. You began therapy in 1973, while Anti-Oedipus *appeared in 1972. Deleuze liked to say that the unconscious is a factory that manufactures desire, that it isn't a theater for giving birth to mom and dad roles. Your book* The Revolution in Poetic Language *appeared in 1974, so couldn't you have gone off in other directions?*

I leave you to choose whether a factory is nicer or more liberating than a theater. But unlike what you're implying, I was receptive to the anarchistic aspiration of *Anti-Oedipus*, and I really like Deleuze's work. When I indulge myself and hand out my own academic prizes, like the media does so much these days, I even think Deleuze is perhaps the most original and radical of contemporary French philosophers. His exoneration of madness, insistence on the paranoiac variants of the *socius* and of the "bind" have particularly interested me. In the wake of *Anti-Oedipus* I was drawn to look into Artaud's work, and to specify how, from his experience of psychosis, he puts the family, God and essentially language into question without trying to get away from them. Instead he constructs, in counterpoint, a new type of inadmissible sublimation. It's a work that destroys tradition to uncover what has been repressed there; it's given an idiolectal voice that is both unique and something you can share in; it's always eternally to come. It's the savagery of the unconscious distilled in writing, culture unmasked and reworked. I looked at the primordial silences in language, the unsaid, i.e. the pre-Oedipal stages that have to do with the mother-daughter relation, this maternal imprint on the psyche and on language—what I call the "semiotic" (distinguished from the "symbolic" which would be the preserve of language, its signs and syntax). But in the course of my own personal work, which was semiological and already psychoanalytic, I saw that since Freud a lot of psychoanalysts had become interested in the "narcissistic" and "psychotic" modes of the unconscious. I also noticed that *Anti-Oedipus* was breaking down an already open door, as far as clinicians were concerned, though not for the public at large: the doors should have been opened with a lot more caution. In the best sense, *Anti-Oedipus* had a mundane liberating effect—publicly liberating, you could say—on familialist ideologies and the normative confinements psychoanalysis can sometimes have. But the book didn't come as a surprise to the kind of psychoanalysis that's careful to rehabilitate the pre-Oedipal and psychotic latencies of the unconscious. I'm particularly thinking of the clinicians who had worked in contact with the English like Winnicot and Bion, following on from Melanie Klein. Now the principal difference between the psychoanalysts of the English school and the French school is that the English accentuate the catastrophic, let's say psychotic dimensions of the unconscious, whereas the French privilege the erotic, i.e. Oedipal dimensions. Does this all amount to saying that Oedipus should be rejected as the shallow depths of psychic life, that any psychic life worthy of the name focuses exclusively on what comes before or after it, on psychosis, in short? It would be absurd and wrong because once you acknowledge the radicalism of the death drive and the destructiveness that an endemic psychosis produces in each of us, you must not forget that the human being is a speaking being, a self in language, in constant communication, bonding. Now invoking "language" and "bond" at once raises questions of limits, prohibition and law; questions that are intrinsic to our condition as speaking beings and which are raised and will always be raised anew. How can one let the forbidden and law modulate our subjectivity while preventing it from becoming a tyranny, a bind, a barbarism? This is the problem. You can't get rid of the question by idealizing madness after idealizing sex. But one has to acknowledge the latency of madness and maintain in relation to it a more flexible prohibition. That's the art of psychoanalysis. It's the art of... art! Here psychoanalysis and art have common cause...

Already in the mid-seventies, did you have the feeling that Deleuze was going too far? Did it threaten you when he rejected the father and preferred fraternal love?

You know, when you've survived Stalinism, not much scares you. Especially not love and desire. At most, they provoke curiosity... My own experience, more specifically my analytic experience, taught me that desire, if it exists, is unalterable, infinite, absolute and destructive. But by the same token, the father is indispensable—source or inhibitor of desire, just like he is... analyzable. You see it today with the resurgence of the sacred. Look at those crowds at World Youth days in search of a good father, kneeling before the Pope who enables millions of people (even in a country like Cuba, ravaged by dictatorial paternity) to "fix fatherhood," i.e. to console themselves in the shelter of a paternal figure who is neither absent nor tyrannical but simply present and loving. Some daring works, like *Anti-Oedipus*, made things easier on themselves by doing away with the effort to think about limits, prohibitions and paternity. As long as left-wing, libertarian thinking deludes itself on this problem of paternity, which is all about law and prohibition, it will be driven to dead ends. Like succumbing to the charms of the Machiavellian, God-like father—Mitterrand for instance. "It's forbidden to forbid" [a May '68 motto] is one of the most cruel prohibitions: it makes you laugh at first but you go crazy in the end. Let's be clear. We have a simplistic image of the severe, tyrannical father, and it's supposed to have been invented by good old Freud. Nothing could be more schematic, though you do find this figure of paternity in the founder of psychoanalysis. For years however, particularly in France, psychoanalysts have been showing up the multiple dimensions of the paternal figure. In *Love Stories*, I was very interested by a note in the *Self and the Id* where Freud outlines "the father of individual prehistory." It's about a loving father who is essentially not the father of prohibition but the father as object of the mother's love, a father who loves, and without whom there would be no ideal. He's the pole of primary identification that consolidates our capacities for representation; he's the storekeeper of our imagination. There are other facets too: the father's femininity, his passion, his desire. Rather than taking on the tyranny of the paranoiac father, it seems more interesting to me to think about a complex figure of paternity. Without that we remain in a hallucinatory mother-child dyad that's beyond civilization. When we're not stirring up the love-hate homosexual fascination between the subject and this father-tyrant...

As far as brotherly love is concerned, sublimating it is what anchors the social bond, and Freud was the first to observe this. Deleuze was very frank about unmasking the sexual tenor of this sublimation. From now on it's not a secret. You even notice that removing the stigma from male homosexuality sometimes leads to reinforcing what is most conformist and repressive about the social bond. So you get American gays proud they're finally allowed to be cops! That wouldn't have gone down well in May 1968; it would have made Deleuze laugh too. But while you're asking me this, what you really could have asked me was whether a sisterly, not brotherly love exists and what its social destiny could be. It would lead us to look at the homosexuality endemic among women, which isn't symmetrical to men's because the daughter's attachment to the mother is its prototype and it is universal. Could this homosexuality provide the basis for a female compact, a more (or less?) dramatic communality? You begin to wonder about that when examining the mores in the harems, for instance. Or what about this other question: assuming that the war of the sexes is structural, is the heterosexual couple the quintessential success story, a kind of miracle of civilization? There are so many puzzling questions but also many promises for the third millennium...

Were you aware of them in 1968?

I was aware that the whole adventure implied the death of God. In the sense of the madman's cry in Nietzsche: "'Where is God?' he cried. 'I will tell you. *We have killed him—you and I.* We are all his murderers. But how did we do this? How could we drink up the sea? Who gave us the sponge to wipe away the entire horizon? What were we doing when we unchained this earth from its sun? Where is it going now? [...] This tremendous event is still on its way, still wandering; it has not yet reached the ears of humans. Lightning and thunder require time...'" [*The Gay Science*, 125] May '68's affirmation of an absolute desire, of "unhindered pleasure," follows from the Nietzschean superman's will to power, and it has nothing to do with "hooligans" or "gang" vulgarity as we've so often been led to believe. It's the opposite: it's about exploring the intimate logic of the will to power or of "desire" and "jouissance," to use the terms of the day. It's about demonstrating that this will or this desire comes from the feeling of a lack, that they are intrinsically will or the desire for power, and that this aspiration intrinsic to power is rooted in the value awarded to life itself, to the extent that life is growth, becoming, process of production. If "God" was one of these Values, or the summation of all others, going against them meant putting God himself (i.e. Meaning fixed as Value) into question. Some of us were aware of the enormous ambition behind this subversion. What was at stake wasn't replacing bourgeois society's values by other ones, but instead contesting the very principle of Value, i.e. power, lack, life as process of production and work itself. Underlying the indictment of "consumer society," it was productivist society and subjectivity that was in the dock. In short, questioning a model of humanity that had absorbed into itself the transcendent ideal (God) and which, from this immanence, was in hot pursuit of "values" and "objects." The *enragés* of '68 bore the possibility of a mutation in metaphysics, a sort of change of religion or civilization that like all upheavals (Nietzsche says it in the text quoted above), takes time to reach people's ears. Often it only arrives distorted, e.g. in a commercial apology for *health sex* or "total-pleasure." Actually May '68 was about relentlessly questioning all values, powers and identities. Not in order to leave a vacuum, but instead to start anew.

How?

To me, the implicit Nietzscheanism of the *enragé* had to give way to reading Heidegger and above all the wisdom of Freud. Note that one of the fall-out consequences of '68, at least for some, was reading Heidegger again, going past the ever-vigilant critique of his compromise with Nazism. The philosopher doesn't condemn the "madman's" rage but keeps it up instead, opening up the way of art for him (when subversion becomes artistic life as well as an "art of living"); art in this case means the memory of thought and care for those who are closest to you. However for me, as for a lot of other *enragés* of '68, Freud's discoveries were best for modulating the subversion of prevailing values. It's in Freud, isn't it, where you get that perennial interrogation-as-revolt, but inscribed in memory and in the recesses of language, an intimacy that opens up the subject's identity towards the other and Being. It's in Freud that Judaism and Christianity are taken up again. What is psychoanalysis, if not this integration of the limit and the law at the core of this transmutation of values? This is what the father brings about in the anthropological sense, and what the "madman" seems precisely to forget. For human beings, this will to power that wants to "drink the sea," "wipe away the horizon with a sponge," "separate the earth from its sun"—isn't it a merciless desire both for and against the authority of the father? To me, psychoanalysis then seemed the logical continuation of the metaphysical ambitions of '68. "We want Everything!" is a cry of desire *and* the death wish directed at the father. This truth proclaimed by Judaism and Christianity makes them indispensable at this current stage of human history. The genius of psychoanalysis will have been to take the power of desire seriously, as well as the truths of monotheism, and to show that they are the inevitable—though variable—conditions for questioning values, and giving human desire its meaning.

On the problem of the father, don't you think that the one of the negative aspects of the legacy of '68 is not having tackled with what Pierre Legendre calls "the death of reference," or the mad pretension of destroying humanity? Is this question of the father making some crazy come back, thirty years on?

If you're going by the media exploitation of '68, he would be right. On the other hand, I don't see where exactly this murder of paternal reference is supposed to have taken place. Let's take the field of analysis, because psychoanalysis has become popular in France in the wake of 1968. Whether they are Freudians or Lacanians, analysts are justifiably bent on rehabilitating the father before they deconstruct his inhibiting or abusive power. Certainly this has to do with the weakening of authority and the break-down of the modern family, but it gets to the point where some analysts, like me, are then faced with the necessity of thinking and identifying the figure of the mother. For the mother is definitely not just a genetrix; instead, she takes on a symbolic and civilizational function that our culture goes gooey over, but says little about, because we're so busy saving the father. Another example: at university, after accusing the professors and a few outbursts of "spontaneous speeches," we lost no time installing new mandarins, as well as reinstating the professorial lecture because it met the students' need to look up to "authorities."

People complain about the wholesale destruction and attribute to '68 the economic crisis and unemployment which ravaged families, especially the least well-off ones. Technology, the influx of immigrants, the shift from a culture of the word to the culture of the image landed the social and metaphysical ambitions of May '68 squarely on the miseries of the triumphant industrial era and then the post-industrial age. Some of these ambitions managed to expand democracy, as we've already discussed. Others were distorted, notably in certain educational circles that prized spontaneity, doing away with memory and the erasing of prohibition. But that's only one reading of the polyphonic complexity that May '68 was, and it's neither the best nor the only possible one. We aren't done with deciphering the message.

We'll come back later to today's paternal function. I'd like to carry on with assessing '68 but before that I'd like to hear you talk about your experience with feminism. How did you experience the women's revolt during and after '68?

It was pretty painful. From the start I was involved in the Psy & Po movement created by the Women's Bookstore. Just before my trip to China in 1973, the group offered me a contract to write my book, *Des Chinoises* (1974, tr. *About Chinese Women*). When I handed in the manuscript, there was no reaction. Then a stormy meeting, in which I got flak for not having valorized female homo-sexuality; for having signed off with the father's name—the husband's name wasn't a better option in the eyes of my accusers, so it was a no-win situation; for not having paid due homage to the leader of the movement, and so on. I wasted no time in leaving a group which seemed to magnify the worst aspects of political parties, sects and totalitarian movements. Although many women found shelter and provisional encouragement there, sexual abuse and corruption scandals quickly erupted... I carried on thinking about the femi-nine condition though, either on my own, or within the context of my academic or clinical work, but I don't consider myself a theorist of feminism. What little I wrote on women is empirical, dispersed, work in progress...

At the end of your book New Maladies of the Soul, *you fervently hope for a civilized feminism opposed to the war of the sexes and careful to establish constructive relations between men and women. You write that you want to "de-escalate the death-match between the two sexes." What do you mean by de-escalate? And why do you absolutely insist on distin-guishing three generations in the history of feminism?*

From its very beginnings, from the suffragettes to existentialist feminists, the feminine movement has aspired to the socio-political equality of the two sexes. The struggle for equal wages and status, the rejection of feminine or maternal attributes, considered incompatible with any incorporation into universal history, derives from this logic of identification, which is universalist from the start. The second phase in feminism, which got seriously involved with art and psychoanalysis, started after May '68. Women think of themselves as qualitatively different from the first generation and essentially care about the specifics of feminine psychology and its symbolic accretions. They don't want "power" because it's considered "macho," instead, they're looking to communicate corporal and interpersonal experiences that have hitherto been culturally marginalized or overshadowed. They aspire to a "feminine writing," a "feminine language," a "feminine cinema," and so on. Now there seem to be signs of a third stage marked by the greater and greater presence of women on the social and symbolic stage. With the stigmas removed, "power" is there for the taking. Yet does it have to be wielded in the same condition, with the tact and obstinacy of the immemorial housewife? Or instead modulated in terms of the specifics of feminine experience, with all the complicity it implies—intimacy, sexuality and those matters closest of all—nature, the child? These are the two versions— universalist and liberal on the one hand, particularist and inspired by May '68 on the other—that are on display in the present debate on "parity" and the more important role of women this parity is supposed to bring to French society. Note also that the decreased militancy of the feminists came about as a result of May '68's subversion of identity, i.e. the recognition of psychic bisexuality, the internalization of the other sex, of the stranger, even of evil in oneself. Less claims are made for "women as women" too, just as any excessive sexualization of the debate now leaves people cold. There's a certain accomplished, mature serenity among this third generation of women; it's pragmatic and dignified and comes from a non-religious "sacred": it has no illusions but it's tough and dependable.

This is strange. You seem to claim the whole heritage of '68—its subversive spirit and radicalism—and reject it at the same time. You defend revolt and prohibition alike, keeping 1968's transgressions and cultural experimentation but rejecting its spontaneity and heady delusions. But in your writing over the last thirty years—notably Sens et non-sens de la révolte *(1996, tr.* The Sense and Non-Sense of Revolt*)—you relentlessly denounce the normalization and* ennui *that afflict our societies. You write: "When prohibition or power can no longer be found, disciplinary and administrative punishments multiply, repressing, or better still, normalizing everyone." According to you, we're not guilty or responsible, but simply incapable of revolt. Can you be more specific on this?*

There is no revolt without prohibition of some sort. If there weren't, whom would you revolt against? We can soften prohibitions, make laws less rigid or tyrannical, tone down the legalism of the United States, the dictatorship of Muslim fundamentalist rules in Iran and so on. But the intra-psychic limit and prohibition are the indispensable conditions for living and for the life of language and thought; the codes of modern democracies can only seek out the optimal social variants of these so they can protect us from aggressive drives and yet ensure their creative exercise all the same.

My question is about prohibition: do you feel that today, postmodern societies haven't been able to preserve its role?

Society at the end of the Twentieth Century isn't lax, far from it. There are lots of places around the world where prohibition is oppressive, where it excludes or forbids, abroad as much as in France. Immigrants have difficulty integrating, not only because they're forbidden access to the national territory (just and humane legislation is slowly being implemented on this), but also because they're deprived of certain kinds of political and cultural recognition; and then, trapped by their claims for identity, they deny themselves such recognition. The unemployed too, forbidden to work and earn a living... These are draconian forms of prohibition, and they don't affect human existence any the less deeply than the arbitrary prohibitions we denounce today in the two totalitarianisms of modernity, Stalinism and fascism.

On the other hand, these depriving or exclusionary prohibitions work alongside a certain permissiveness both in family contexts and in relation to moral codes. I realized, as other colleagues did, that our patients had changed, that we weren't observing exactly the same psychic discontent that Freud had diagnosed. So I talked about "new maladies of the soul." These new patients are suffering less from repression or inhibiting prohibitions than from the lack of reference points, such that their psychic apparatus hasn't really established itself: they're having difficulty representing their internal or external conflicts. If ultimately the point of the psychic apparatus is to make a *camera obscura* inside which these internal and external aggressions are inscribed, verbalized and symbolized, so as to defend the subject from these attacks, well then, with the new patients, this defense is down. When psychic representation is in default, it takes the form of psychosomatic illnesses, drug abuse, or acting out—from botched actions to perverse violence, like pae-dophilia and social vandalism. What can't be represented is abreacted in a violent act or else goes deep down inside where eventually everything self-destructs—organs, self-awareness and life itself. What are the causes of this destruction of psychic representation? They're many. Firstly, modern human isolation: automated and computerized work prevents affective interaction with other people and subjects people to the imperatives of abstract procedures or regulations. Secondly, the ruined family unit, where the father's absence or his diminished authority goes along with the unavailability of the mother, if not her depression. Thirdly, the weakening of religions, or their worldly or fundamentalist return, has eroded educational and moral benchmarks. It has left mostly unregulated child training, the control of sphincters, sexual differentiation as well as matters of social hierarchy and behavioral codes—table manners, respect for adults and the elderly and so on. Finally, the "new world order" confronts us with the fluctuating "authority" of banking capitals, or rather with their virtual scripture; compared to this, the authority of the politician is a fiction and, increasingly, a caricature. Authority can be provisionally salvaged during a war or by the integrity of a visionary character (de Gaulle), exceptional political and cultural savvy (Mitterrand) or moral rigor (Jospin[17])... Very easily though, they succumb to the brickbats of a media fond of character flaws (Clinton). Exit the Hero—our leaders aren't idols, and who's going to complain? It's not May '68 that devalued power, it just crystallized a phenomenon already underway by revealing its consequences for each individual and for the social order.

You can't deny this crisis, and many people deal with it by relegating the "events" themselves to an archaic romanticism. As if society's present lull—which is rather forced and precarious, because of globalization—had absorbed the crisis for which May '68 represents the extreme and liberating symptom. It would be more clear-sighted to see it as an extended symptom and look for an adequate therapy for it. Particularly by the transferential bond: it inscribes into the patient's psyche both the limit that is the analyst-other, and the optimal prohibitions you have to respect to understand the sense of his interpretation. The result is that you are initiated into law and otherness, insofar as they are the intra-psychic conditions for the constitution of an "interiority," i.e. a subjective intimacy that allows the patient to acquire a psychic autonomy and only through that, confidence, desires and a capacity for creation and challenging things. At a less personal level, associative life can teach a respect for flexible prohibitions, those that ensure both protection and the possibility of a new start for each of us. But also through contact with other cultures and other religions, which, like certain polytheisms, apparently avoid concentrating prohibition on the sole figure of the father, distributing and modulating them across complex social and cosmic hierarchies.

Would you say that demanding happiness, pleasure and jouissance was an unhappy utopia of '68?

Not at all. Don't confuse me with those gloomy souls who recoil with horror when confronted with the aspiration for happiness, decrying it as a miserable utopianism. The Romantics went in for this nostalgic denigration after the French Revolution, and all the dynastic restorations kept on in the same vein. Let's stop this, for pity's sake, and let's try to go along with this radicalism of subversion. I am going to use a vocabulary that may shock people, but it can allow us to size up this phenomenon. Infinite jouissance for each person at the intersection of happiness for all... is it anything else but the sacred?

This sacred isn't the stability of religion nor the institution that inhibits it to some degree or other, but something that cuts across all that and allows our most imperative bodily needs to access symbolic representations that could be shared and that are sometimes sublime. This transition from the body to meaning, from the most intimate to the most binding happens via sexual desire. And a lot of religions recognize in sexual climax the core of their conceptions of the sacred. Others, like Christianity, only admit it by denying it, preferring to go the way of idealization and sublimation. The demand for happiness, which all revolutions in modern times harbor, has never been simply a demand for economic happiness—more bread for the poor. It's an immediate claim for sexual and spiritual liberty, an adjustment of private and public pleasure, and as such, it implies a modification of the previous conception of the sacred. A sacred that is no more and no less than the most singular gratification intersecting with the constraints of the community—balancing pleasure and sacrifice.

The 1789 Revolution knew that when it claimed happiness for the individual *and* for the people it was overturning prior notions of the sacred. The "new regime" wasn't shy in promoting a new spirituality, and so it clumsily and abusively translated the apologies for passion so dear to the Enlightenment. Misery and Terror put an end to this spiritual revolution. May '68's subversion plays a part in prolonging this mutation of *homo religiosus*, and it would be wrong to believe it fixed once and for all within the stratified hierarchies of Hellenism or Judeo-Christianity. With the progress of technology and our needs increasingly satisfied, the second half of the Twentieth Century has made the claim of an infinite happiness possible and compatible with the family and the nation—as long as you transform them. Does that mean root and branch, anarchically to a degree, but carefully too? That depends. But let's emphasize that those who want to "have boundless pleasure" and head off to sanctuaries in some church or temple, using them as the sole, unique enclave of their interior experience, still don't destroy the family and the nation. Although there were religious revivalist tendencies, notably for Oriental ones, the French movement was less religious than the American. It was looking to achieve private jouissance, not "in private" nor even away from the world, in the extra-territoriality of religion, but in the public domain, extended from the family to society and to the nation, while demanding that it made itself receptive to the right to singular and absolute jouissance.

The right to allow jouissance in the public arena, isn't that a contradictory demand?

First of all, let's note that this false dialectic sanctifies the public domain to such an extent that its most violent critics don't devalue it, but are confident instead in its capacity to satisfy the right to individual jouissance. At least so long as society violently calls itself into question and is ready to accommodate individuals and their singularities. "We're realists, we want the impossible"... What was at stake indeed was achieving this impossibility—the reality of jouissance. Precisely because it is intrinsically impossible, we'll achieve jouissance in a constraining society, provided that we subject it to fervent and sustained disruption. While it's true that this critical appeal launched at the public domain misunderstood what "impossible" or "prohibitions" actually meant, it really did help loosen up social constraints—now you talk about "civil society," creating "networks," and so on. Part and parcel of the search for a new happiness—the equivalent of a new sacred—is the devaluing of *homo faber* in favor of *homo ludens*; this is something else May '68 called for. It's the first time in history that human beings, in a collective, rather than aesthetic or religious show of strength, allowed themselves to question the absolute value the "worker" had become in industrial society. Marx himself, well-known gravedigger of capitalism that he was, never went so far as to envisage the decline of the world of work, except in a hypothetical and paradise-like communism. Not merely abolishing consumption, but further down the road, the valuation of work itself, effectively amounts to an unprecedented transmutation of values—no less radical than the ambition of the Overman. It is possible to see this as the superficiality of irresponsible people, a "utopia," as you say, of anarchists or spoilt children. More fundamentally, I think, May '68's radicalism bears witness to a indefinite sense of mutation in the essence of man, the search for other forms of the sacred (in the sense of a fine-tuning between the body and the soul, public and private, which is what I suggested above). The thirty years that followed these demonstrations have covered or obscured them, but they're still there—the crises of postmodern society attest to them. Globalization is a long way from providing the optimal solution.

I don't quite understand the link you're making between happiness and the marketplace. Half the time, isn't leisure a form of stultification that enslaves minds in the name of mass culture?

Where do you see this link? I'm talking to you about the sacred, and you're talking about the marketplace! Happiness in terms of jouissance is the antithesis of happiness as the satisfaction of consumer needs; it's actually one of the main features of May '68 and yet a lot of people criticized it for that, accusing it of unfortunate irrealism. The call was for the sacred, not for luxury living; it can still be heard, despite the technocratic and automated appearances of the new world order: it's there in the popularity of religious sects. Was this appeal too stark, too precocious? So we hadn't realized that unchecked industrialization was endangering the environment. Nor understood that the need of the impoverished masses to acquire consumer goods was making the marketplace more desirable than the "joy of freedom." OK, but thirty years after, limits are being put on time at work, certain people are talking about "economic horror," we're paying more attention to leisure. Are these things stultifying? Is popular culture an enslavement? Sometimes, but not necessarily, and it just depends on those carrying out these initiatives to resist consumerism and make mass leisure pursuits not just sites of pleasure, but also sites of awakening and questioning.

The Chinese proverb goes: "The bonze is an idiot but teachable." The "masses," as you say, aren't any the less so—let's not lose faith in the Internet for this.

Do you think that this rebellion of workers and young people in 1968 can be passed on? Does the spirit of '68 belong to the French revolutionary tradition or simply to a twitchy baby-boomer generation?

When I was preparing my class on Hannah Arendt, I realized she doesn't react to the events of May '68 very much at all. But when she replied to Mary McCarthy's scandalized letters (for her part she very hostile to so much pretentious disruption), and despite her concern for her husband's health, Arendt was nevertheless interested in Daniel Cohn-Bendit, the son of very close friends, and wanted to contact him. In her *Essay on Revolution*, Hannah Arendt is very critical of the French Revolution and its terrorist populism; she prefers the legal dimensions of the American one. From the outset, however, she says something that is apparently in contrast with her "liberal" image, and particularly as she is the fierce critic of the French Revolution: "It's worth betting that the spirit of the French Revolution will survive and that, in the centuries to come, it will be right." This phrase chimes bizarrely with the words of Jean-Paul Sartre, whose political positions Hannah Arendt criticized. Sartre said: "We are right to revolt." In fact, by taking totally different routes, Arendt and Sartre support what I try to defend in my own works on revolt —*The Sense and Non-Sense of Revolt* and *La Révolte intime* (1997): that revolt is indispensable, both to psychic life, and to the bonds that make society hang together, as long as it remains a live force and resists accommodations. That's what we perceive as a "sacred" and it assures the possibility of a human group's "survival," possibly even the survival of the human being itself, says Arendt.

There is a passage I like very much in We're Right to Revolt. *I'll summarize it rapidly: Philippe Gavy asks Sartre why he's persevering with writing* Flaubert *rather than going down in the street and writing popular literature. Sartre replies that it's useful for thinking. Gavy persists and asks him what thinking means. And Sartre answers: "To think is not to be in the movement."*

We agree: to think is to revolt, to be in the movement of meaning and not the movement of the streets...

Was one of the aporias or contradictions of the '68 heritage that most of those who were in the movement, as Sartre said, also became corporate leaders? (It's the theme of Generation, *Hamon and Rotman's book.) They are newspaper bosses, publicity chiefs, lawyers, and so on. Sartre, who was naturally obsessed by what the "young men of 1848 became," notes this contradiction straight off in very ironic way. Is this contradiction part of our heritage?*

I think Sartre finally let himself get intimidated by Gavy or by others. For he stopped writing, even as he was carrying on with *Flaubert*, which had now turned into a dissection of the writer, damning and admiring him in equal measures. After *The Words*, fiction, imaginary activity, seemed like a neurosis you can get rid of, notably by choosing to serve the people's cause. It's a pity for Sartre, since novel writing can be a vigilant and tireless source of critique, whereas political engagements of the most generous sort can be stultifying—even for someone as nauseous as Sartre. It's also a shame for the people who I think are better "served" by *Nausea* than by the *Critique of Dialectical Reason*. As for the leaders of May '68 who became business executives, it only goes to prove how difficult what they were calling for actually was. The sacred isn't compatible with blind automation. But, after all, what do you know about their personal experience, even if they are "corporate executives"? Besides, I'd point out that this '68 generation in France also favored a post-Heideggerian philosophy elaborated on questioning and deconstruction, rather than on thought as calculation; it experienced psychoanalysis and introduced it into the human sciences as well as quite broadly into the practices of mental health; it got involved in the anthropological study of so-called "savage" societies and also China, the Arab world, Judaism and so on. These are hardly conformist investigations.

How did this new idea, i.e. happiness is for any revolution, specifically take shape in 1968? At the time, was there not in this claim for collective happiness a sort of communitarian myth, a second-rate Fourierism[18]?

I have already dealt with this question. The will to join private jouissance to public happiness isn't necessarily communitarian. It responds to the need for social ties, which, along with the acknowledgment of prohibitions, is a condition of psychic life. The resurgence of religions and sects reflects this anthropological constant, whatever the perverse manipulations that go with it. May '68 was ahead of its time here too, bringing out by its very excess the crisis of *homo religiosus* which still is ongoing, and maybe won't find any stable resolution, contrary to what happened in the past. With the difference that in the French movement, sexual experience was thought through, analyzed and theorized by way of psychoanalysis and Enlightenment materialism. This approach favored a non-religious sacred, a kind of radical atheism which is perhaps the only non-vulgar or dogmatic form of atheism: exhausting transcendence in its own terms by liberating speech through erotism. I'm thinking less of Fourier than of Georges Bataille.

This need for an absolute that you're talking about is a theme of Arendt's. Is it typical of '68 or of every revolution?

Arendt saw the absolute of the eighteenth century's revolutions as a radical break with the past; liberty for all is an idea unknown before the revolution of 1789 and it introduced in the course of social and political history the Christian event *par excellence*, namely: "renaissance," "beginning," "renewal." Kant showed that these notions constituted the essence of Liberty as "self-beginning." Arendt could have said, along with Condorcet, that "the word revolutionary only applies to revolutions that have liberty as their objective." But she thought that revolution (particularly the French Revolution) substituted the necessity of economic welfare for the struggle for freedom, so that the poor people's thirst for material goods blocked freedom, and this led to the failure of the Revolution. I think she underestimated the fact that in France, more than elsewhere, "happiness" doesn't just mean getting rid of poverty but access to an "art of living," cultivating erotism and taste, fulfilling the spirit and the flesh. That's what jouissance means. Also, this jouissance must be possible not only within the family, at work or in Church—valued spaces certainly, but not that much—but it can and must happen in the city. Here's the feature that makes the French the closest of the moderns to the Greek ideal: blossom in a public place.

The crisis of May '68 is definitely not outside this tradition, but it adds two unexpectedly paroxystic traits. On the one hand, limitless individual desire and the wager that it's compatible with the happiness of others. On the other hand, the challenge to society itself as a stable, productive entity, an economy, a "management." You'll note that I'm talking about the "crisis" of May '68 and not about the "revolution" of '68. The instant act of revolution has always needed to cleave to institutions that will realize it in the longer term, and they end up betraying it, either in the French or Russian Terror, or in legalism American-style.

With May '68, this logic entered another phase, one of continuous subversion and the propagation of revolt. The term "permanent crisis" suits it better, because it covers the mistakes as well as its failures and relapses. It also indicates that this revolt is historially grounded: it's concerned with the monumental history of mentalities and not exclusively with the linear history of political regimes and modes of production; it indicates that no institution can bring it to fruition, but that we're now in an era that continually questions identities and institutions. This is the kind of thing you could read in a May '68 publication, *De la Misère en milieu étudiant* (*Of Student Misery*): "Revolution has to be reinvented, just like the life it promises." What I take from this "phraseology" is a perception of vital and uninterrupted process. What is more, the frequent use of the word "play" [or game] is understood in a ludic and guiltless sense. Hence: "to enter the game of revolution" through self-managment...

"I rebel, therefore we are": that's how Camus formulated the modern version of the *cogito*, in terms of the challenge of daily life. He meant the new solidarity achieved through an awareness of one's discontent and through the subversion of stable values. This is where the "we" part comes from. But it's a placid and definitive "we are," as opposed to revolt that's simply taking its course. Rather say: "I revolt, therefore we are still to come." If we don't keep this possibility open, the indefiniteness of the revolt May '68 represents, there is nothing left to do but to submit to the all-encompassing power of calculation and management that perpetuates the end of history.

Does this calling for public happiness in 1968 seem excessive to you today?

It's the done thing in France today to devalue the public domain. Certainly, we all know how much schools can lag behind the real needs of society, hospitals behind the modernization of care and services, how Air France drags its feet on competitive prices, and so on. It is urgent to modernize the public domain, so why not privatize it? But that's not the real question. France has made the public domain into a myth; that makes it a rare, if not the sole inheritor of the "public" [*res publica*] in the Greek sense of the term. It has nothing to do with the socio-economic realm supposed to oversee the production of what, in the past, was the family scene, but public in terms of this meta-familial entity, the nation, and Europe too, eventually. This notion of the public not only takes us beyond family limitations, but also beyond the logic of business, which begins by protecting and stimulating but ends up with the closed system of supply and demand. That kind of "public" is simultaneously a means of social improvement and a refuge in times of distress and depression. I don't see how its importance in France would be a consequence of '68. It follows from the nation's history, the foundation of the Republic's self-reliance. I recently attended a debate on public service inside one of our most important public ministries. I was really surprised to see that its "servants" were the bitterest critics of the public domain. Maybe it was constructive criticism, but perhaps they were expressing what is depression on a truly national scale, public as well as private. No, I don't share your mistrust of the public. It's the opposite, actually, and even taking into account the extensive reliance on law, you can detect an appeal for a renewal, really, of politics itself. This kind of politics would be fairer, sensitive to people's singularity, without condemning them to isolation; just the opposite: it would show them generosity, recognition or forgiveness. Isn't it a sign of this bond's vitality that we would look for this response or recognition not in a temple or simply in the workplace but in public places? We entrust what is most sacred in our possession to public institutions. If there is a danger, it is not to be found in the cult of the public as such, but doubtless in over-rigid judicial procedure, dithering over modernizing the public sector and associating it with the private or the international domain, with new technologies... All these adjustments can go hand in hand with the rehabilitation of public life, if what you mean by that is a political life of contestation and permanent scrutiny. That's the spirit of '68. And French society is very sensitive to it, perhaps more than others—proof of its maturity, hardly its outdatedness. "I revolt, therefore we are.... still to come."

WHY FRANCE, WHY THE NATION?

Integration Is Not Possible for Everyone □ The Myth of National Unity □ The French and the Americans □ National Depression and Manic Reactions (Le Pen) □ Politics, Religions, Psychoanalysis □ Taking Refuge in France

"Nowhere are you more of a foreigner than in France. The French haven't the tolerance of Anglo-Saxon Protestants, the accommodating insouciance of the South Americans, or the German or Slavic curiosity that rejects and assimilates in equal measure, and so the stranger confronts that daunting French sense of national pride [...] And yet, nowhere are you better off as a foreigner than in France. Because you remain irrevocably different and unacceptable, you're an object of fascination. You're noticed and talked about, hated, admired, or both." You wrote this in Etrangers à nous-mêmes *(1988, tr.* Strangers to Ourselves*). Do you still feel a foreigner in France, thirty years after coming here?*

Of course. It's a paradoxical situation, because abroad I am taken as one of the representatives of contemporary French culture, whereas in France I am and always will be a stranger. It's normal: it's a question of language, mentality and perhaps a certain personal marginality that writers have always claimed for themselves, like Mallarmé. After all, he wanted to write "a total word, new, foreign to language."

Why didn't we read or hear from you during the (still ongoing) affair of the illegal immigrants? Aren't foreigners' rights in part your domain, not to mention open, respectful rights for migrants?

I haven't signed petitions for a long time now. I believe that a psychoanalyst can make certain aspects of her personal life appear in her written work since we analyze with our entire personality. Moreover, "new patients" suffer from a real lack of interest in their own psyches; the imaginary experience of the analyst can reawaken that interest and pave the way to the subsequent work of dismantling and interpretation. On the other hand, taking up a political position can inhibit the patient's freedom, curb and censor his or her own biography. When I talk about politics, like I'm doing now with you, I try to express myself carefully. It's impossible when you're a militant "sounding off." Beyond that, much as I am sensitive to the distress of the immigrants, equally I don't think it's desirable to give the deceptive impression that integration is possible for everyone who asks for it.

Right now, the movement for the immigrants without proper papers is virtually isolated, even if some centers making claims for them are still active. The Chevènement document gave those foreign Africans reason to believe they can obtain what they request by get-

ting their names on the administrative lists. Around 160,000 of them are asking to be given citizenship. Personally, I think that they should be, since they have been working in France for years. What is your own opinion?

Each individual's case is examined carefully at the present, it seems, and I have no reason to doubt Jean-Pierre Chevènement's intention to give legal status to those who have been working for years now and meet the criteria agreed to by the majority of the French.

You write in Le Temps sensible *(1994, tr.* Time and Sense*) that Proust is one of the writers who has best explored the clannish nature of French society. You say he got to "the heart of the social game." What did you mean by that?*

Proust was very sensitive to the "clans" that make up French society. He suffered by them, while trying to be part of one. He was the first to diagnose it in a way that's both droll and agonizing: the French, he said, transformed Hamlet's declaration "to be or not to be" into "to be in or not to be in." Could social awareness compensate for what is, all in all, a metaphysical restriction? But all that socializing, military strategy and salon play-acting, just to get himself accepted, or just to exist, work and get his work acknowledged! Until the end of his life, Proust sought to win over the various clans, to appropriate society's collective trance. Looked at this way, this fin-de-siècle dandy was the first writer who didn't shrink from the "society of the spectacle"—the salons, editorial offices, publishing houses, soon television... His attitude during the Dreyfus Affair was very significant. He defended Dreyfus right up until he realized that his supporters were forming an equally corruptible group by themselves, and furthermore flawed by an anticlericalism eager to close the cathedrals! Proust didn't trust any clan, whether it was a High Society, or literary, political or sexual ones. In *Sodom and Gomorrah* he writes, "Let's leave to one side for the moment those who [...] want to have us share their tastes, who are doing it [...] with apostolic zeal, like others who preach Zionism, Saint-Simonism, vegetarianism and anarchy." To go against the group and the gregarious instinct, you have to write in the mode of the fugue, compose cruel and ridiculous "impressions" that shock and are most effective at dissolving clannish associations. They are the conditions of that particular experience, writing itself, as the search for "pure embodied time" and of the "book within." Not above clans, nor without them, but through them, at their margins, in order to bear witness to them. "Whether it was the Dreyfus affair or the war, each event provided writers with other excuses not to decipher this book, they wanted to secure the triumph of the law, restore the moral cohesion of the nation, hadn't the time to think about literature" (in *Time regained*). This irony, aloof and complicit at the same time, endows Proust's texts with a pained clear-sightedness about the Society circles, salons and social classes, and it made him exceptionally attentive to the clannish instinct that entrances individuals.

Is Proust out of the ordinary in this?

Proust is unique and few writers after him dared imitate him or comment on him. He is always impressive, when he isn't terrifying. Some still dismiss him, calling him "little Marcel" and accusing him of having turned the novel into poetry, and killed it off as a result! Who are the great writers that came later who paid homage to him? Mauriac and Bataille, both attracted by Proust the mystic and the blasphemer; Blanchot who detected the "emptiness" in the cathedral that is the *Recherche*... No, there aren't that many. Céline is fascinated by him, but just rejects him more completely as a rival supposed to have only written in "Franco-Yiddish"...

Would you say that today's French society is as clannish as it was at the beginning of the century?

Yes, and I'll say exactly why. France is one of those countries where national unity is an essential historical realization that has an aspect of myth or a cult. Of course, each person belongs to his family, a clan of friends, a professional clique, his province etc., but there is a sense of national cohesion that's anchored in language. It's an inheritance of the monarchy and of republican institutions, rooted in the language, in an art of living and in this harmonization of shared customs called French taste. The Anglo-Saxon world is based on the family. Certainly, in France, the family is an essential refuge, but Gide could still say: "Families, I detest you!" There is an entity above and beyond the family that is neither the Queen nor the Dollar but the Nation. Montesquieu said it once and for all in the *Spirit of the Laws*: "There are two sorts of tyranny: one is real, consisting in the violence of government; the other is the tyranny of opinion that makes its presence felt when those who govern set things up that go against the way the nation thinks." Everywhere this "way of thinking of the Nation" is a political given, it's a source of pride and an absolute factor in France. It can degenerate into a prickly and xenophobic nationalism, and we have many to testify to that in recent history. You would be slightly mistaken (to say the least), if you didn't take this into account. What is more, this cohesion has a tendency to fragment, so that you get networks, sub-groups, clans, each one as specious as the next, and all rivals, generating a positive and entertaining diversity as much as a pernicious cacophony. Chamfort already said it: "In France, there is no public or nation because rags don't make up a shirt." What you can minimally argue is that rags remained prevalent under the Fifth Republic—the different parties all know quite a bit about that!

Proust described all this well: the Verdurins, the Guermantes, the professional circles, sexual ones... Many meta-families that are initially liberating, enabling talents and vices to flourish, art to blossom, freeing up political debate and personal behavior, but then they close in on themselves just as quickly in order to exclude the person who doesn't submit to the clan's rules—for being too personal, too free, too creative, like the artist, the Jew, the homosexual... This is the sadomasochistic logic of clannishness: we like you as long as you are one of us but we expel you if you are yourself. It's impossible to "step out of line" (Kafka), "society is founded on a crime committed in common" (Freud). Proust shares a lot with Kafka and Freud, but he's more funny; he doesn't display his chagrin too much, doesn't set up a program of therapy, doesn't ever withdraw into personal isolation or into "art for art's sake." He plays the game the better to laugh at it, laugh at the clan, at society, at oneself.

Outside society, no salvation. Unlike the Americans, we can't be reborn in the desert...

No salvation outside society? I wouldn't say that, because you should add that we immediately create clans when jokers appear to put other people's sense of humor and endurance to the test, society's too... The French all want to be jokers like d'Artagnan: nothing to do with Dostoyevski's tragic joker, nor with the Protestant conquerors chasing Moby Dick, managing their fish factory with the Bible in their right hand...

Jean Schlumberger said, "France will be in a state of dialogue for ever. I doubt, I know, I believe—take away one of these three assertions and France falls apart." Do you find dialogue in France is a bit stifled these days?

Dialogue the French way isn't intended to establish a consensus, but to surprise, to reveal, to innovate. It can seem disconcerting, and I've often felt that myself after a talk, for instance. French people listening to me go up to the mike and tell me that not only do they do it better than you but they're doing something different entirely. Americans, on the other hand, ask real questions, they want to know essential truths, like whether your believe in immortality. I start off preferring the Americans' naive curiosity but in the end I get taken in by the dialogue of the deaf that the French carry on, because it uncovers insolent, often interesting characters. And, anyway, psychoanalysis tells us that there is no dialogue, just desires clashing, forces colliding. From this point of view, the French are maybe more mature, more knowing than others.

That said, the political domain is designed to harmonize these conflicting desires and incompatible forces. Is this balance more lacking in France than in other countries? Frankly, I don't think so. The French like appearances, like to show themselves, to show off in public, let other people in on how bad they're feeling or what the state of their bank balance is. At the same time, this exhibition of unease doesn't mean a total concession to media spectacle: one doesn't believe in it so much, one remains mistrustful, not really taking it seriously. The French are impressed by the media, of course, but don't allow themselves to get caught up in a Monicagate or an O. J. Simpson trial. Although they like spectacle, the French make fun of histrionics.

As for national pride, it can become Poujade-like arrogance and a lack of enterprising energy: the French aren't open to Europe and the world, and are content to cultivate tradition as a consolation. But it also offers aspects that are real advantages in this post-industrial age. For the "people"—the people of Robespierre, Saint-Just and Michelet, I mean—poverty isn't a flaw. Sieyès spoke of the "ever unhappy people," Robespierre was pleased that the "wretched were applauding me," Saint-Just's conclusion was that "the destitute are a world power." Is it any wonder that the people on minimum wage and on welfare make their claims heard? More than in other countries, they have a sense of superiority because they belong to a prestigious culture. They wouldn't exchange that for the temptations of globalization, not for anything. You'd say that's a pity, because the French will stay uncompetitive and lacking in enterprise. Even our students are hesitant about studying abroad, while we have a lot of foreign exchange students, eager to come here and learn. But a lot are beginning to realize it and are making up for the unbalance. On the other hand, this sense of dignity, i.e. taking away the guilty stigma of poverty and valuing the quality of life, is an increasingly welcome new perspective for both developing peoples and the people of industrial countries feeling oppressed by automation, inhuman hours, unemployment, lack of social security and so on. Clearly, when this proud and demanding entity we call the "people" addresses itself to the public authorities then the dialogue that one would wish for turns into an open confrontation. For all that, though, I still don't think the channels of communication are blocked. But what if we took at face value popular demands to redistribute national and global wealth? It would be a precedent that would make other countries sit up and take notice...

I find you optimistic, because it's very often grandstanding theatricals that overshadow what is really and intellectually at stake...

I find you pessimistic. In what other country would you find the intellectual stakes more fundamental and more in the spotlight? Really! Just to stay in my own field: we have opened up a debate on modern psychoanalysis and its relations with neuroscience and politics that you don't have in any other country. I have just come back from a conference in Toulouse where 800 people stayed on afterwards from 6 to 11:30 that evening to discuss the detective novel and new maladies of the soul, asking fascinating questions on literature, mental health, the evolution of the family... I really don't find the French half-asleep or theatrical.

Yes, but doesn't that explain a real absence of historical perspective in contemporary debate?

The grand historical perspectives, as well as the great challenges in history, are a function of their time, and you can't ask a globalized industrial society to follow the models of the last two centuries. The dichotomous logic of the great men and intellectual figures who fight obscurantism and power in anticipation of happier tomorrows has given way to a more complex situation. There's no use in looking for a Jean-Paul Sartre going up against Charles de Gaulle, Voltaire against the King. In our period of transition and endemic crisis, what counts is rather the questions than the answers. Just like it is in psychotherapy, the truth of "historical perspective" would be to let new forms of questioning come in, instead of proposing solutions to meet the anxieties of the person under analysis. Modern revolt doesn't necessarily take the form of a clash of prohibitions and transgressions that beckons the way to firm promises; modern revolt is in the form of trials, hesitations, learning as you go, making patient and lateral adjustments to an endlessly complex network... That doesn't prevent prospective ideologies from appearing to satisfy the psychological need for ideals and seduction. But we know better now where to put them in their rightful place—as actors in the Spectacle.

What are the ways open to us?

The nation, for example, which we mustn't leave to the National Front . It's a common denominator that many people need, and we still need to separate what's best about it from what's worst. The idea of the people has to be protected from Poujadist and Le Penist conceptions, and safeguarded as guarantor of generosity and a culture of jouissance—the very opposite of anodyne globalization.

How do you explain the new dimension the nation is taking on these days?

I'm going to rely on psychoanalysis to answer you. Depression is one of this century's commonest maladies, particularly in France. A recent statistic showed that our country is one of those where suicide deaths are the highest, fourth in Europe behind Finland, Denmark and Austria (not counting the ex-Eastern bloc and China). The causes of depression are complicated: wounded narcissism, inadequate maternal relations, the absence of paternal ideals, and so on. They all make the subject forget how important it is to make connections: initially language (a person who is depressed doesn't speak, he "doesn't believe" in communication, wraps himself up in silence and tears, inaction and immobility), and ultimately connections to life itself (it ends in the cult of death and suicide). More and more you sense that today individual depression is also the expression of social distress: losing a job, longer and longer-term unemployment, problems at work, poverty, lack of ideals and perspectives.

Above and beyond individuals, you sense that France is suffering from depression on a national scale, analogous to the one private people have. We no longer have the image of a great power that de Gaulle restored to us; France's voice is less and less heard, it has less weight in European negotiations, even less when in competition with America. Migrant influxes have created familiar difficulties and a more or less justifiable sense of insecurity, even of persecution. Ideals or clear and simple perspectives like the ones the demagogic ideologies used to offer—and they are no less tempting—are out of place. In this setting, the country is reacting no differently than a depressed patient. The first reaction is to withdraw: you shut yourself away at home, don't get out of bed, don't talk, you complain. Lots of French aren't interested in community life and politics, they aren't active, gripe a lot. And then what do you do with French patriotism, a crowing arrogance that is part of our tradition? It's a too easy contempt for others, an excessive self-assurance that makes them prefer to forget the world outside and avoid going to the trouble of undertaking something worthwhile. Today the French are both boastful and self-deprecating, or lacking in self-esteem altogether. What is more, a person who is depressed has tyrannical ideals, and it's his draconian superego demanding a supposedly deserved and expected perfection that, at bottom, orchestrates the depression. I formulated this hypothesis in 1990 in *Lettre ouverte à Harlem Désir* (tr. *Nations without Nationalism*). Since then, this malady has had moments of growth and decline, and we were at rock bottom before the "dissolution" of Parliament in 1997. Still, as a result of the subsequent elections and the real or perhaps simply promised economic upswing, the French mood is visibly improving. But that latent depression hasn't gone away despite everything.

What does the analyst do faced with a patient who is that depressed?

He begins by restoring self-confidence; you do this by rebuilding both their self-image and the relation between the two partners in this cure, so that communication can begin again and a real analysis of this unease can happen. Similarly, the depressed nation has to have the best image of itself that it can, before it can be capable of going ahead with European integration, for example, or industrial and commercial expansion or a warmer reception of immigrants. It's not about flattering the French, nor trying to foster illusions about qualities that they don't have. But it's the nation's cultural heritage that isn't stressed enough, which means as much its aesthetic as its technical and scientific capabilities, despite such a lot of justified criticism. Particularly guilty of this are intellectuals: they're always ready and willing skeptics, quick to push Cartesianism to the point of self-loathing. Giraudoux wrote: "Nations, like men, die from imperceptible discourtesies."

I wonder if our generosity to the third world, and our cosmopolitanism hasn't often led us to commit imperceptible discourtesies that aggravate our national depression. It's time to attend to it. For if depressives commit suicide first, they find consolation for their pain by reacting like maniacs: instead of undervaluing themselves, lapsing into inertia, they mobilize, sign up for war—holy wars, inevitably. Then they hunt down enemies, preferably phony ones. You'll recognize the National Front and integrationist movements there.

Ernest Renan said: "The nation is a daily plebiscite, just as an individual's very existence is the perpetual affirmation of life." To a greater or lesser degree, the nation is a historical unit born out of conflict. Making these conflicts come to the surface isn't an easy thing to do for the kind of individuals we are.

When contemporary psychoanalysis encounters these "new maladies of the soul," what shows up are failures to work out psychic conflicts. It gets to the point where not only are some people today incapable of telling good from bad (both become banal as a result—Hannah Arendt had already seen that happen during the Holocaust), but for many, their psyches can't represent their conflicts for them (in sensations, words, images, thoughts). And so they're laying themselves open to vandalism, psychosomatic illnesses, drugs. Conversely, you could say that modern society also offers spaces and occasions to try to remedy these deficiencies. Society has explicitly delegated psychoanalysis to the task, representing one of these opportunities individuals are offered to work out their conflicts and crises. It sort of takes over from politics and religion, which were traditionally the proper places for the expression of our conflicts. It has to adapt itself to historical change, be more involved in society's debates and not turn its back to the media, but above all build new bridges with the human sciences, medicine and neuro-psychiatric research. More broadly, civil society is trying to find new political ways to allow its conflicts, for too long stifled by an excessively centralized national administration and political parties, to show up and develop. Associative life, which seems to be developing better and better, could be this new version of the nation: it could offer a unifying public space that provides a sense of identity, memory and an ideal—working like an antidepressant, in so many words. At the same time, it would multiply contacts between individuals, providing care geared to the diverse demands made on it.

In the talk "Europhilia, Europhobia" you gave at NYU in November 1997, you say: "Before you undertake a real analysis of its resistances and defense mechanisms, it is important to restore national confidence in the same way you would restore narcissism or the ideal self in a depressive patient." Are you confident about national self-confidence?

I trust the respect for public space, the capacity to take away the stigmas that surround misery and the exercise of solidarity in the face of it. But also the pride in cultural heritage and the culture of jouissance and freedom. I distrust the attraction of "the good old days," nationalism (which isn't the same as the nation) and sexism. But I've already gone over that, so let me say a bit more about what I'm personally confident about.

Even if a nation defines itself in terms of its ties to blood or soil, most base their image of identity on language. It's particularly true for France. The history of the monarchy and the republic, given their administrative cultures, the verbal code, and their rhetorical and pedagogical institutions led to an unprecedented fusion of national and linguistic entities. It means that literary avant-gardes have to be more subversive and extremist in France than anywhere else, just to disrupt this protective layer of rhetoric. Those avant-gardes are severely marginalized or abolished during a time of national depression, invariably met by a retreat behind set ideas about identity. There is then a cult of traditional language, or "French good taste" that shores up a failing or even unrecoverable sense of identity.

The foreigner, who is always a translator of sorts, hasn't much of a chance in this kind of context. Of course, there have always been Jewish courtiers and foreigners admitted to the the Académie française. But these alibis, which flatter the national conscience, shouldn't mask the basic tendency: just like the avant-garde's daredevil feats, those who dare to incorporate themselves into an "other language" are met with suspicion and quickly fall victim to ostracism. It's easy to understand why in France people who are the most shrewdly nationalistic, the most insidiously xenophobic set up and exercise their power in the institutions that oversee literature studies. He or she who speaks the "other language" is invited to be silent... unless he or she joins one of the reigning clans, or one of the rhetorics that hold sway. Naturally, she or he can also try to leave the country, to be translated abroad. Actually, the fate of the outsider is open by definition: perhaps that's its salvation in the end...

When I come home to France after trips to the four corners of the globe, it sometimes happens that I don't recognize myself in these French discourses, despite the fact that it's been my only language for 30 years now. They are discourses that look the other way on evils, on the world's misery and instead applaud the tradition of irresponsibility—when it's not nationalism—as the sole remedy to our century. For alas, it's not the glorious seventeenth century, nor the century of Voltaire, Diderot and Rousseau... After a day of psychoanalysis sessions—where there's a place for real speech, even if it is dysfunctional—there's nothing worse than reading or meeting some journalist or other punctiliously serving up the stereotypes of stylistic and philosophical protectionism. French excels in false praise, in hollow enthusiasms, in heady eulogy of those who are "one of us." It's more resistant to hybrid versions of itself, unlike English, and it's not interested when it comes to adding new things to the language, unlike American, which constitutes a new body of language, nor even Russian, despite everything. French today has a tendency to be satisfied by an untranslatable authenticity. All in all, it's a temple, and certain institutions and organs of the press—more than writers themselves, by definition nomadic and scorched souls—are trying to wall it in. If the outsider gets worried, starts talking or criticizing, he is accused of disparaging France. Frenchness hardens into a region-alist stance, and, like in Aeschylus's time, only allows outsiders one discourse—the humble supplicant's...

What did you think about getting rid of military service?

You're bringing me back to serious matters. I totally approve of getting rid of it. I'm going to make a confession: I've always detested military service. I've never understood why some of my female friends, when I was a little girl, wanted to be boys. The mere idea of military service made a choice like that awful.

From a republican point of view, doesn't it shock you that we're getting rid of something that was after all a place (like school too) of social mixing?

Do you seriously think military service is the only place for social mixing? Frankly, though I'm convinced patriotism isn't passé yet, I still think there are other ways of cultivating it— scientific, artistic or sporting competition, for example. As for social mixing, public schools and universities are appropriate places. In a modest way, I'm taking part in a rethinking of how higher education is organized; among other things, it includes a possible fusing of the *grandes écoles* and the universities. It's definitely not about taking away from the excellence of the former or the generosity of the latter, but allowing a better mix. In a civilian context—for it doesn't have to be necessarily military—there are other, similar activities you can think of, like helping the disadvantaged at school, in the so-called fourth-world and so on. They're activities that develop a real concern for others, i.e. love and caring. That's what "public service" means, doesn't it? To serve, care for, preserve, revive? Caring, like a basic degree of love, is also a powerful anti-depressant. "Service"—OK. But "army"—no. It's not my thing... But don't you think you're overdoing it a bit, asking me all sorts of questions, as if you take me for one of these intellectuals—though they don't exist anymore—who has an answer for everything? From military service to theories of the Big Bang—why not while we're at it?

People have been talking recently about reintroducing lay morality in schools. Do you think we should teach children to love their country?

Why not? But a sense of "my country" as a reserve of memory or an imaginary limit, rather than in terms of a religious foundation or an ultimate origin. So you would go in search of the past, and get a sense of being different from others. A memory and limit that one would love: it's a long march that may give love itself a new flavor. It would be a more internalized and sober sense of love.

What is a successful transfer?

For me, it would be just like analytic transference. This implies that there is a separation: at the end of my analysis sessions, I leave my analyst. My inhibitions and censoring mechanisms are relaxed, I'm in touch with my unconscious drives and my creativity increases; it is a state of autonomy that makes me capable of freedom and choice, far beyond what my analyst has transmitted to me right there and then (literally). In short, a successful transfer is one you can question and modify, one that stimulates the creativity of the "disciple."

At the same time, you recognize that you can't master what you're conveying?

That goes without saying. If the two extremes are dogma and just anything goes, what a good "master" conveys to his disciple is both a set of literal meanings and a sense of rigor. And at the same time an ability to question, make new beginnings, re-births.

Don't you find it a shame that we've got rid of the oath-swearing ceremony that confers nationality?

It seems logical to me that children born of foreign parents raised on French soil, educated in French schools and speaking French, get French nationality without having to ask for it. You would put the matter differently for new-comers.

Yes, but there isn't the symbolic act of commitment. It's a formality. It's not symbolic, or ritualized. There is no civic oath…

I attach a lot of importance to ritual because it harbors an irreplaceable symbolic potential. I have been very touched by the ceremonies of American or Canadian universities, especially when they have elected me to honorary doctorates. The elections also include the students: there is a tangible recognition of their status as intellectual individuals, their integration into a national and international academic community and into the symbolic memory of their school. This tradition has been lost in France, or it's pretty perfunctory. I try in vain to revive it, and it just earns me pitying smiles. People tell me that the French have too good a sense of humor to go along with all that playacting. That remains to be seen. You could think of rituals adapted to this ludic spirit: for example, if we're talking about the university of Paris Denis-Diderot, where I teach, it could borrow from the symbolism of the Encyclopédie, and include the arts and poetry, as well as a party of course...

"If we are only free subjects insofar as we are strangers to ourselves, it follows that the social ties shouldn't associate identities, but federate alterities." You wrote this in the journal L'Infini. *Can you be more specific on that?*

Following on from Rimbaud, psychoanalysis makes us admit "I is an other" and even several others. Overturning the traditional notion of a person's "identity" is in the same spirit as the "deicidal" movement I was talking about in the context of May '68. If God becomes a stable Value, if the Person coheres into a stable identity, all well and good, but all the energy of modern culture is directed against this homogeneity and tendency toward stagnation—what it exposes instead is fragmentation. Not only are we divided, harboring within "ourselves" alterities we can sometimes hardly bear, but this polyphony gives us pleasure. This is enough to threaten facile morality and compacted entities. Consequently, it's not surprising that a lot of people are giving twentieth-century culture a miss, don't want to open their eyes and see the actually troubling truths all that reveals. However, by recognizing this strangeness intrinsic to each of us, we have more opportunities to tolerate the foreignness of others. And subsequently more opportunities to try to create less monolithic, more polyphonic communities.

What do you mean by "federation"?

An accord between polyphonic people, respectful of their reciprocal foreignness. A couple that lasts, for example, is necessarily a federation of at least four partners: the masculine and the feminine sides in the man, the feminine and masculine sides in the woman. I dream of a public and secular space in France that stays committed to preserving the "general spirit" dear to Montesquieu, but wouldn't erase the foreignness of each of the constituent parts of the French makeup either; it would federate, respect and unify them instead. And this is neither a neutralizing incorporation into a larger universal whole nor English-style communitarianism that breaks the "general spirit." All in all, it's a subtle balance we haven't yet managed to put into practice.

Outside France and its culture, what are the countries you feel closest to?

Greece is my cradle; my homeland, Bulgaria, is a part of old Byzantium. I'm writing my next novel on it—it's another detective novel but this time on the Crusades. I feel close to the Russians, because of the melancholy and carnevalesque sensuality of the "Slavic soul." But I get the strongest impression of civilization from Italy and Spain. By way of reply, I'll read a few passages from my novel *Possessions*: "Many fall in love with Italy, and I have too: its profusion of beauty that perpetually astonishes one, an excitement akin to serenity. Others desire Spain: it is haughty because it is unreasonable, mystical but nonchalant. As for me, I have definitively taken refuge in France [...] I lodge my body in the logical landscape of France, take shelter in the sleek, easy and smiling streets, rub shoulders with this odd people—they are reserved but disabused and possessed of an impenetrable intimacy which is, all things considered, polite. They built Notre-Dame and the Louvre, conquered Europe and a large part of the globe, and then went back home again because they prefer a pleasure that goes hand in hand with reality. But because they also prefer the pleasures reality affords, they still believe themselves masters of the world, or at any rate a great power. An irritated, condescending, fascinated world that seems ready to follow them. To follow us."

THE DISORDERS OF PSYCHOANALYSIS

The Art of Psychoanalysis □ Mother and Lover □ The War of the Sexes and Latin Libertinage □ The Feminine and the Sacred □ The "French Distinction" □ Fighting with Grace □ Women Psychoanalysts □ *Jouissance* and Tenderness □ A Civilization of Love □ Resisting Uniformity

"Today, and still more in the future, I think psychoanalysis is the art—I admit the conceit—of allowing men and women who inhabit modern, arrogant, polished, expensive and exciting cities, to safeguard a way of life." You wrote this in 1988. Would you say that one person in therapy is worth two that aren't?

Why stick at two? Like schizophrenia or when "one splits into two" as recommended by Mao in his Little Red Book? Your figure is way off, because the person in therapy isn't two, but legion—diabolical, in other words. Everything's possible then: you become saint or sinner, cynical or tender. But in every case, and not in a frivolous sense, therapy loosens your inhibitions and defense mechanisms, and by restoring infantile memory and the potential of the drives, it stimulates creativity. The end of the psychoanalytic process is a moment of mourning, but the end comes with new capacities for love and changes in your professional life. I don't put people under my psychoanalytic microscope. Old Sigmund goes back on the shelf once I leave my office, because the analyst only comes into existence when called upon. But I note that people who have had therapy—even when it's more or less complete, by definition it's never really over—are perfectly lucid about their maladies and limitations, as well as those of others; it makes them receptive, expectant, mobile. In the best cases, of course. There's a specific kind of humanity that gets up off the therapist's couch, though, attentive to its own and other people's revolts.

"Making babies is fine, but having them, what an iniquity!" That was what Simone de Beauvoir said, borrowing Sartre's quip for herself. Maternity seemed incompatible with her freedom to create and live as she wanted. You're not one of those who finds motherhood a handicap—quite the opposite...

Beauvoir's reaction betrays her own personal situation and that of the period as a whole. It was a serious mistake for feminists to oppose those who are creating children and those who are creating in work-oriented senses. Sure, the two tasks are difficult, and they're impossible to reconcile if the economic conditions aren't right and if the desire for motherhood is either lacking or has been distorted. By emphasizing professional life, even if it's indispensable, feminists have neglected the most important civilizing vocation of women, and that is maternity. But they shouldn't be incompatible with each other. The effort to reconcile the two experiences leads to difficulties and dead ends. We'll come back to them. But let's note first of all that since the Virgin Mary we don't have any other discourse on motherhood. It's a strange mix of physiology and biology, cells and significance. Women give life, men give it meaning: that's what they used to say. That's all changed. Women also give it meaning. Have they always done so? Perhaps. Your language is also your mother tongue, and it's aptly put, for without an "adequate mother," no child will ever have spoken at all. We agree on that. But mothers are doing it more and more, which isn't to say better and better, though sometimes it works like that. Add to all that genetic manipulations and other cloning: we'll need male cells, and it doesn't matter which ones, but you can't do without eggs. Whatever the horrors of science fiction—not all so fanciful actually—it seems that the future of our species depends more and more on women. It depends on our capacity as women to reconcile sexual and professional freedom with the wish to give life and guide it towards meaning.

Would you go as far as to say that a woman who chooses not to have a child is incomplete?

Absolutely not. Some women—and some men—manage a "symbolic maternity" in their professional and personal lives, particularly in teaching and in the caring professions, though not only these. What I call the maternal vocation isn't the work of the genetrix or the pregnant mother—in itself extraordinary—but rather a special magic: as desire modulates into tenderness, it brings you from biology to signification and thus into representation, sense, language and thought. The woman-mother's drives are re-routed, so that instead of being satisfied by an object of pleasure (essentially a perverse object), the woman/mother's drives are not inhibited, but deflected onto an *other* rather than an *object*—an other to care for, protect and love. By the lover and mother's psychical magic, the perverse object of desire is aligned with the other or transforms itself into an other. We're at the dawn of otherness, and civilization. We know too well what accidents can happen on this journey: the narcissistic appropriation by the mother of her offspring—when it is no longer an other then, but her own prosthesis—over-possessiveness, vampirism, abuse, all sorts of score-settling. And I'm not about to forget the bondage of devotion, the masochism of selflessness, and so on. But beyond all that, maternal experience is fundamental, for each person of either sex, not just for the ones who have given birth. We're afraid of it. Some denigrate it, starting with women themselves. You get the "heifers," the "wenches" Céline describes, the women who "spoil the infinite for us." Others are paranoid about its malevolent power—those all-powerful witches and matrons. Those who censure it open the way, more or less knowingly, either to the ongoing automation of our species ("everything is in our genes or in technology, the maternal instinct doesn't exist, mothers neither") or to the return of religion to fill the vacuum (friends from Scandinavia have just told me that books on the Virgin Mary are all over the book displays and dominate the bestseller lists). But I'm definitely aware of the real challenge, which is managing to do both things at once, i.e. lead a professional life and a life as a mother. Even if they aren't actually succumbing to serious psychic illnesses, a lot of these "superwomen" are still clearly exhausted. In *Possessions* I described myself as a headless woman. The wounds, deprivations and suffering women suffer today—as simultaneously lovers, workers, wives, mothers—have crystallized themselves for me in the image of decapitation... Have no fear, though, I also pictured myself as an investigative journalist: I'm a woman who inquires, who can and does want to know...

"It's important that the fundamental difference between the sexes be drawn more precisely, truthfully, and less on the terms of the media. Feminism had the great merit of making that difference painful, stimulating both surprise and symbolic life in a civilization that is just bored unless it's at war or speculating on the Stock Exchange." You said that in 1979. To read you (and gauge the difference between eras), you sometimes seem to hesitate, on this question of sexual difference, between dramatization and reconciliation. You give the impression of intensifying the war of the sexes while all the time hoping for peace. How do you situate yourself in relation to that?

I don't hesitate for a moment on this point, in any case. What I say is that the war of the sexes is endemic but we can still transform it into communal living. They're the two sides to the same coin, not something I would hesitate about. The difference between the sexes means that our impulses, desires and mentalities differ and very often diverge. Men and women don't take the same pleasures, and don't expect the same benefits from a relationship: some are more active, some more passive, some more centrifugal, some centripetal. Fortunately, psychic bisexuality compensates this overly schematic dichotomy, and makes a more or less healthy agreement possible. Besides, the economic dependence of women has long forced them to bend the knee, to give in on everything. The result is that the war of the sexes didn't take place. But it's taking place right now in the United States, and it's pointless for us to mock the American feminists' aggression, their lawyers' greed, the media's vulgarity, because it's not clear that our refinement as Latins and Europeans can protect us in the long run from this very same barbarity. If you could hear what is said on the therapist's couch, it's a lot coarser than pillow talk. Thanks to the feminist movement, what became both self-evident and painful to bear was the psychoanalytic truth that says there is an antagonistic difference pitting the sexes against each other—it heightens desire, but also turns desire into sado-masochism. It's not about stopping just here. Civilization, like love, like the couple, is about continuing the war by other means, until the war gives way to a perpetually self-renewing harmony...

Is there something distinctive about the French? A French way to tackle sexual difference?

In the Ancien Régime, there is a prestigious tradition of sublime women who were products of aristocratic easy living, the trans-gressive license of Catholicism, and such a sophistication of conversation and writing that it also became a way to real knowledge—Mme du Châtelet, Madame de Sévigné... This strain continues all the way up to the first intellectual, Madame de Staël—writer, philosopher, political thinker—and lasts on in the fey sensuality of Colette. And there's the courageous and trenchant intelligence of de Beauvoir. But the bourgeoisie has tended to check this emancipation, shutter women behind ideas of maternity and morality, make her an adjunct to business, or "affaires." As Mona Ozouf has brilliantly shown, even the French Left, from the Revolution to very recently, wasn't par-ticularly encouraging. It was just the opposite: we were too afraid of the priest, the "friend" to women who prevented them from acquiring secular minds, who cloistered them away in the

Church. It partly explains why recent feminist movements, after May '68, were cool toward political parties, notably the parties of the Left. But deep down, French culture isn't puritan, and this Latin libertinage, this pagan wave of Christianity, gives French women a confidence that is far removed from the clamorous bitterness of the Anglo-Saxons. I have just finished trading letters with Catherine Clément on *the feminine and the Sacred*, where I insist on the fact that even the Virgin—her above all—went beyond a consoling role; she also had one as protector of women's sensuality and power, for all that she is decried as a symbol of repression and denigration of the female body. Mary, after all, is mother of the arts and queen of the Church. In short, because they seduce, because they're mothers and partners, French women don't really feel they're being trampled on. Are they wrong? Perhaps they are lagging behind sisters from other countries and not getting into positions of political power quickly enough. Without a doubt, and we're going to try to sort that out. But this unhurried pace is also the sign of a certain balancing of the relation between the sexes, specific to the "French distinction." You notice two things distinguishing French women, in their latest cultural incarnations, from "modern women" from other countries. First of all there is joie de vivre, seduction and pleasure to the fore, as opposed to complaints and perpetual claims-making. They acknowledge a lack of well-being, are fully aware of the failure of couples, the burden of household chores and the no less heavy ones at work. However, the best way of combating them isn't by getting bogged down, but to go about things with grace and coquetry. What's strangest of all is that many manage it. French women fight, but with a smile on their faces. It makes a change from the depressions and ill-humor of the New York or Muscovite women.

Next, the desire to preserve and cultivate this feminine difference, rather then transforming ourselves into clownish clones of the macho men both envied and combated by so many strict feminists, goes hand in hand with the recognition of what I would call a common measure for the two sexes. In France there is a ground where we can all live and work together, men and women, beyond and with our differences. Is it the result of French universalism, that taught us we're all of the Human race before being men and women? Perhaps it comes from this culture of the Word, for that distinguishes French culture from others; every person, from the poorest to the most privileged, excelling in it as both a duty and a pleasure. Perhaps it is a culture of the word that shows us to be all subjects to the same "common denominator," i.e. subjects of the word and its symbolism. Recently, thinking about the very specific contribution made by women psychoanalysts to the modern development of psychoanalysis, I observed that French women psychoanalysts have certainly made important contributions to our knowledge of childhood and psychoses—the archaic domain, in so many words—like their sister colleagues in other countries. But more often the French shed new light on Oedipus. Now who is Oedipus but the common denominator of the two sexes? They recognize universality in him whilst looking for the specific way the two sexes relate to one another. And last but not least, they provide very subtle analyses of pleasure and female jouissance, on how it modulates into tenderness, and also on its perversions. In other words, it's psychic activity's solar face: you'll get burned, but at least it all happens in the light of day.

Are you for parity?

Initially, I was bothered by the paternalist and victim symbolism hidden behind this demand for parity: by claiming parity, you implicitly acknowledge that women are pariahs, and you paternally decide to redress the balance. But it seems impossible to counter sexist obduracy without such an emphatic claim. Up to now, I have been talking about the positive aspects of sexual difference in France, but I'm quite aware of the hatred that a woman with a body and a mind can inspire. Did you see the hunters' demonstration? Campaign machismo exists and who would hold back from manipulating it? So parity—yes! But for what? Quickly answered, the question is the renewal women could bring to political life; their not just being content to become super businesswomen.

So the difference between the sexes should be rediscovered, and certainly not abolished...

Give this difference force and content. Let women express themselves. So they don't really want to assume political responsibilities? Maybe they want another kind of politics. What kind? What kind of love, family and procreation might this involve? What measure of personal space, kinds of responsibilities; what kind of meaning do you give life when confronting desire, technology? Whether it leads to a massive arrival of women on the political stage or not, "parity" could be an occasion to rethink politics in terms of the anthropological stakes politicians tend to forget...

It's as if you were making women—and perhaps also men— guardians of the incommensurable?

We return to the themes of May '68. When the infinity of desire and the infinity of jouissance were confronted with the limitations of social arrangement, it led to a redistribution of the Sacred. A "Sacred" introduced into the very heart of politics. This question is still open, and what is called "women's problems" simply restates the question in a particular way. For the woman subject is positioned, more dramatically than a man, on this knife-edge between life and meaning that goes beyond the social: that's what I called the Sacred. Don't you find it extraordinary that all this can become the topic of public debate in France? It's a sign, amongst others, of a very precious conception of liberty that we should protect at all costs. More and more the modern world has gone over to a cult of freedom to adapt to circumstances. To be free means being successful at adapting to the logic of causes and effects that governs a world that transcends us. And it's a given that the transcendence we're talking about is no longer, or not only that of an impalpable religious morality, but a very pragmatic one of production and the market. It's a great success, and who wouldn't buy into it? Surely not the impoverished inhabitants of Manila who ransacked supermarkets on the day of the stock-market crash. But we are also inheritors of another freedom, and perhaps the "French exception" assumes that freedom with the most conviction and skill. Before any beginning, adaptation, undertaking or success, freedom consists in revealing yourself to the other. I present myself to you: I and you, man and woman, and every other difference besides. In perception and speech, we experience our similarities and incompatibilities, and in revealing them we reveal ourselves, and that's how we become. Why is this revelation a freedom? Because it reveals myself to me (man or woman) if and only if I manifest myself or uncover myself before the other (man or woman), and vice versa, each one in their particular differences that go way beyond sexual differences. It reveals me while liberating me, by continually delivering me from what will be me in front of you and you in front of me. What greater liberation is there than this infinite revelation of the self? And these philosophical meditations are in no way abstract, for they're the crux of the debate between man and woman, they demonstrate our concern for another freedom, besides "free enterprise"...

Doesn't that amount to reactivating a kind of civilization of love?

Of course. While it's currently attacked, with neuroscience and behaviouralism coming to the fore, what is forgotten is that psychoanalysis is an experience of the co-presence of sexuality and thought, and an experience of love. Psychoanalysis discovered how much acts of language and of thought are at the interface of sexual development and they depend on the advances or accidents of desire or the drives. Sexual desire isn't a reductive whim that biologizes the essence of humans; actually, it guarantees the intersection of biology and thought. When Freud made this discovery, the psychoanalytic cure he devised was based on the love between people. Transfer/counter-transfer is nothing else than a loving relation between patient and analyst. It's a love story, just as I described it in *Histoires d'amour*, that stimulates the drives and awakens old desires, developing them both at the core of the new loving bond between analyst and patient. All from talking, confiding, naming, idealizing, getting angry, rebelling—in both love and hatred. The analytic experience is a truly experimental love that takes up that loving bond where its antecedents left off (from Plato's *Symposium* to the *Song of Songs* in the Bible to Christian charity, Romeo and Juliet, and the fatal amours of Sade, Baudelaire and Bataille). Desire moors itself to the ideal, and that moderates their respective cruelties. The boundless nature of passion, like that of the ideal, is geared to our accepting our limits. Fundamentally, doesn't love restore the well-being of the unassuming?

Does Lacan's actual skepticism about family life carry less weight in psychoanalytic circles? Has there been progress on this question that allows us to glimpse the possibility of a new thinking on families—and not just reconstructed families—that would make us less pessimistic than he was?

I don't think psychoanalysts are prisoners of Lacan's judgments; they try instead to be receptive to the new symptoms new patients are showing. In fact, the role of the father has changed in modern families; single-parent families are multiplying as well. A lot of couples aren't married and accept the risk of less stable ties to each other, etc. We have already talked about the fact that the father often assumes his own femininity as much as certain tasks traditionally assigned to women. With all this, however, the paternal function hasn't lost its importance: the third element is always structurally necessary to separate the child from the fusional dyad with the mother, to map out primary identifications and stake out the entry into the realm of the symbolic. But this function seems to be changing: these new ambiguities are showing up on the psychic map of young people, those public opinion is calling symptoms of immaturity, i.e. tendency towards regression, narcissistic complacency, borderline or perverted latencies. What the positive version would be is a more developed analogical thinking, a less inhibited imaginary...

I would also insist on what foreign patients have to teach us as far as the new modalities of the paternal function are concerned, i.e. those who speak French as a second language and who come from a far-off culture or religion. One such female patient from North Africa, for instance, suffers from a father's tyranny so destructive that it has literally effaced the role of the mother and of the woman for her. This patient has no image of her mother's face, and can only have sado-masochistic relations with men, which are necessarily violent and demeaning. An important part of her therapy consists in rehabilitating her mother, i.e. relating to her analyst—who is a man—as a good mother, before being able to meet a man she can love and finding feminine ideals in French women. The instability of reference points in migrant communities —something else which shows how problematic and urgent the paternal function is—indicates specific problems among foreign patients, whatever their cultural and religious origins. Thus changing language often doesn't just respond to a political urgency, but is the sign of a matricide that no satisfactory relation with the father could prevent or compensate for. I mean matricide as a violent, destructive separation from the mother that follows on from maternal violence itself.

Exile often harbors a trauma that's difficult to confront and elaborate on; it predisposes these patients to actings-out that run from cynicism to corruption, defiance to fundamentalism. It's difficult to talk about it in public because the matter is politicized from the start, and the symptoms themselves have a complex, partially political etiology. But we are beginning to tackle it head on, conscious of the fact that whatever the eventual outcome of migration, it's not going to be a foretaste of paradise on earth—far from it. We're paying a dear price for the lack of reference points.

Do you agree with Pierre Legendre's definition that "a father isn't an extra mother but an imitation—he gives birth too."

Not really. The father is guarantor of the symbolic realm and I don't think it can imitate gestation. It's about a new regime, a leap into psychic representation the child makes by way of the depressive phase (separation with the mother), identification with the loving father of individual prehistory, which it then consolidates with Oedipus (the trial of castration and phallicism). Also, the formulation you quote supposes a very Lacanian dichotomy according to which the mother is in some ways a hole, when she's not being a phallic mother, and that the "symbolic" only comes from paternity. The father is the guarantor of this symbolic function but there is still a maternal—let's call it a "semiotic"—function. It prepares the future subject for its initiation. My conception of the mother is in terms of a woman essentialized as tenderness but also as a lover who desires, and they're both fundamental aspects of the "second birth," i.e. the birth of the child as subject. The father gives birth, it's true, but in a pretty metaphorical sense: he ensures the "paternal metaphor," finishing with this transfer of drives to meaning that the mother tirelessly prepares for.

Out goes Paul Claudel's strict father, the savage rebellion of the young Cioran or Louis Aragon—you've explored that like no one else. Your analyses have been very attentive to this literary revolt, which goes by way of language and creation, but beyond that, what possibilities do you envisage for our modern or post-modern democratic societies? What social, political, philosophical possibilities do you see that could give shape and substance to prohibitions?

Your question seems to suggest that these literary or aesthetic revolts could be secondary: interesting, yes, but decorative. So we should pass on to social revolt. I don't agree at all. I even try to show, in *The Sense and Non-Sense of Revolt* (1996) and *La Révolte intime* (1997), that what we classify as an aesthetic activity is the true life of thought. Which is to say, thought vivified and incarnate in the desiring body, rather than just a set of calculating operations. The surrealists, like Breton or Aragon, say the same thing. Aragon declared for example: "My business is metaphysics." Or, "What I call style is the accent that man gives to the flow of the symbolic ocean he echoes, who universally mimics the earth through a metaphor." And Breton: "In the world at the moment there are a few individuals roaming around for whom art, for instance, has ceased to be an end in itself." And this: "Love will be [...] that we'll reduce art to its most simple expression which is love." Take Sartre's theater, the way he explores the image as a locus of freedom (in *L'Imaginaire*, 1940, tr. *The Psychology of Imagination*) or his fiction, atheism, and what he calls that "cruel and long-drawn-out" work which exhausts transcendence in transcendence itself (in *Being and Nothingness* but also in *The Words*, etc.). Or else Barthes' semiological interpretation, looking behind the neutral facades of ideology and *belles lettres*. Here is powerful writing simultaneously enacting social revolt. The "social revolution" turned its back on that very revolt, with its relentless questioning, sense of anxiety and very Augustinian message: *Quaesto mihi factus sum* (I have become a question to myself). As a consequence, the political and social "revolution" forgot about the freedom that had brought it about in the first place; it betrayed itself by turning into dogmatism, terror and totalitarianism.

So I think it's indispensable not to freeze "social revolt" in its essence by disassociating it from the life of the mind. But by the same token, I'm not sidestepping the burning issues that concern us today. For example, the necessity of insisting on the "French exception" really isn't about justifying laziness, but resisting the social or cultural uniformity globalization has in store for us, defending that other version of freedom, the art of living and civilization we were talking about earlier. It's about recapturing the fullest meaning of that entity we call "the people." It's not necessarily old-time populism, but a question of suffering, misery, solidarity—the manifold emotional guises of a beaten-down humanity, the one the "plural left" is laboriously trying to reintroduce to political life. Nor should we leave out our common denominator, i.e. the "general mind" which is the bedrock of the French Republic. For beyond the individual, clan, region, religion and so on, it is our symbolic anti-depressant and the haven for every sort of otherness. It's about defending culture as revolt, a culture that upsets and protests, with everyone in on it, from the avant-gardes to the unemployed. And this should be an addition to culture-as-entertainment or culture as "show," rather than necessarily against it. The media doesn't kill the mind, as has been said, and we all like to have fun, but we also want to be able to say no.

IT IS RIGHT TO REBEL...

A Weakened Capacity for Revolt □ Revolt Different from
Revolution □ Calling Things into Question □ Freedom as
Revelation □ The Need for "Authority" □ No Master-
Thinkers □ Feminine Melancholia □ Women's Place in Revolt:
Hannah Arendt, Melanie Klein, Colette

*According to you, the culture of revolt is under threat. Is this a his-
toric failing? Is it linked to the end of the century, or is it due to our
lack of invention? When you go beyond Freud—who made a theme
out of the absence of transgression—the references in the two books
you wrote on this are to twentieth-century writers, but they're not
our contemporaries, strictly speaking.*

First of all, this incapacity to rebel is the sign of national depression.
Faltering images of identity (when they're not lacking altogether)
and lost confidence in a common cause, gives rise at the national
level to just what the depressed individual feels in his isolation:
namely, feeling cut off from the other person (your nearest and

dearest, neighbors, politics) and from communication, inertia, your desire switched off. On the other hand, people who rebel are malcontents with frustrated, but vigorous desires. The subversion they desire can even be a sign of the eroticization of thought—a psychic vitality Thanatos can't negate. Depression can take the form of hyperactivity: certain people or nations remain perpetually agitated—like the cleaner who doesn't stop cleaning the windows—but that still wouldn't necessarily imply a vital society's victory over a morbid one. All the same, you have to understand my formulation more as sounding the alert as than as a diagnosis. Our capacity for revolt has been weakened more and more; it has been altered but not extinguished. It has weakened because of this mutation in technological society we've already talked about, and in which the forbidden either doesn't exist or has become more complex. And at the same time subjects have been abolished or have become multiform. Who do you rebel against if nothing is forbidden, or it has become so complex that you wouldn't know where to start? And who'll rebel if human people are either undervalued or don't value themselves either, or where the self has fragmented so you can't bear it? Even in certain documents of the European Union, it seems we don't talk any more about "citizens," "subjects," or "persons," but "Patrimonial Persons," i.e. we're only taken into account (and that's the right term for it) as owners, and in a new development, not only as owners of material goods (a few centuries of accumulating stock have gotten us used to this actuarial definition), but as owners of our organs. So much the better, you'll tell me, because there are countries where a person doesn't even own his own organs. Well, sure. But you see how impossible it is for this Patrimonial Person, who has become defined by the material goods he may eventually possess and the price-tag on his organs, to live as a free subject who evaluates, scrutinizes, questions and puts himself on the line.

But what do you mean exactly by revolt?

I work from its etymology, meaning return, returning, discovering, uncovering, and renovating. There is a necessary repetition when you cover all that ground, but beyond that, I emphasize its potential for making gaps, rupturing, renewing. Rebellion is a condition necessary for the life of the mind and society, but it's not true, surely, that the conditions that produce a rebellion like that are merely situations where there is no notion of the forbidden, or no simple one, in any case, and when "Patrimonial Persons" get depressed, suffer "new maladies of the soul." Because it's off to the wrong start, then... Contestation isn't the only form of revolt, though. The history of the last two centuries has gotten us used to understanding "revolt" in the political sense of a "revolution" that confronts a Norm and transgresses it by a Promise of paradise. You know what happens afterwards. We have to get back to the intimate well-springs of revolt—in the deep sense of self-questioning and questioning tradition as well, sexual differences, projects for life and death, new modalities of civil society and so on. It's about re-rooting the self that takes us nearer to revolt in the Augustinian sense—*se quaerere*, i.e. put yourself on the line to reciprocally stimulate memory, thought and will. But there is also revolt in the psychoanalytic sense: Freud's insight means an invitation to revolt (anamnesis, desire, love and hatred) all the better to reveal oneself (to create and re-create the self). Understood in these ways, revolt takes on forms that are themselves more complex, less immediately transgressive. Modern automation makes us assimilate technology, but to face up to that, you reconstitute memory, interpret the present and the past; you question, and practice the art of appraising the values that surround us; there is the logic of the game to be added (not opposed) to the logic of argumentation. Narrative, fiction, pictorial and musical creation make up these other, apparently minor facets of revolt, but that's how they are all the more insidiously and efficiently part of the modern world. Literary experiences we talked about are the same thing.

Does your activity as an analyst make you privilege individual revolt and revolt against the father—as you find it in Aragon and Sartre, for instance—rather than social revolt?

I repeat: it's by banking on the individual microcosm, by rehabilitating and valorizing it, by restoring pride in love, desire and revolt, that society has a chance to avoid ossifying into the mere act of managing business. Without that, the only promise we have is the freedom of simply adapting to the laws of production and the markets. We shouldn't keep away from such a daunting perspective but rather counterbalance it by safeguarding and perfecting the most precious of what occidental culture has produced: Duns Scotius' "haecceity," singularity. So no, it's not necessarily intimate individualism, or narcissistic egocentricity that I am talking about. Although it can be, and everyone knows that the world of writers and artists can be a circle of small-minded interests and petty bickering. Perhaps what is most seductive about the "French exception" is this concern for intimacy cultivated by literary experience; it's what should be included as the primordial objective of politics beyond and against globalizing liberalism. We ought to seek quality of life in this demand writers are making instead of in hunters' marches, shotgun and a bottle of red wine in their hands, against Europe, the Greens, women and ducks.

So much for the hunters. For ten years there have been forms of direct action (targeting AIDS and unemployment, aiding immigrants without documentation) and a desire for media visibility. Revolt can no longer take place except in a direct, untimely way; it subsides pretty quickly, but it's still real.

It's both imperative and inevitable that new protests (against unemployment, on behalf of AIDS organizations, etc.) should go via the media. I'm quite critical of intellectual circles whose purism keeps away from any "compromise with the media," as they say, although I am myself pretty mistrustful of journalists. They have their clans too, and I'm not comfortable with their means of expression. But you have to learn without letting yourself be overwhelmed or without ducking the real, basic work to be done—just use it, that's all. Be aware that the image can become an honey trap for the kind of rebellion I'm trying to rehabilitate as a form of scrutiny. And that has nothing untimely about it, nor is it direct, as you say; instead it unfolds, flexible, internalized, problematic. Initially, the media spotlight—it seduced the unemployed or anti-AIDS militants—is spectacular and charged with meaning, but the effect is diminished by the directed aggression of advertising spots, and ends up in more and more television channels, viewers zapping from one to the other. There is nothing better than words, above all words to deepen and sustain debate. If the image isn't subservient to the word, it just reduces meaning into stereotypes. Should we despair? Perhaps. I prefer to observe that we are still at the beginning of a generalized spectacle, that some (still an elite, but it's getting bigger, and hurrah for the elites when they aren't just thinking about their privileges) are beginning to, well, talk up; they're not letting themselves get taken in. At the time of the December 1995 strike, a patient said to me: "It was a good strike, but we've not found the words." That's where we are. When Lionel Jospin was elected, he evoked the necessity of a change in civilization. There hasn't been a lot of talk about that project lately, don't you think so?

There's no doubt that this civilizing value implies what you call the development of thought co-present with sexuality, i.e. the co-presence of sexuality and thought in language. On this subject, which you've made your own, would you say that today, compared to the sixties, there has been progress or regression?

It's still difficult to take stock of this century's end. A lot of people are frightened by it. Both versions of totalitarianism, the Holocaust, Hiroshima. There's a lot to feel ashamed of. It's also the century of an immense labor of thought. I come back to the start of our conversation, to this subversion of values that philosophers, artists and writers, and then psychoanalysis and young people have carried out in public: a radical mutation in the very essence of Humans, insofar as they are religious. We still haven't measured the extent of these advances nor what that rupture means for our usual behavior, for our need for security and identity. A cruelty has come to light: it's the back-cloth of freedom, jouissance, creativity itself. This is the flip-side of this version of freedom as revelation. Artaud was one of those who put it best and one who felt it most dramatically. Men and women come out of it with the feeling that they're irreconcilable. Each in their innermost, and one in relation to the other.

But they also come out of it with the will to make links both with, and then beyond this irreconcilability. So, faced with this "epochal" turmoil, these last years we've been living are administrative fall-back positions: we're tending to our wounds, sacrificing a lot as well, and weaving the computerized spider's web of computer networks, virtual worth, automation. Technology creates comfort, just for some perhaps, but it's objectively increasing for a growing number of people. Only the nostalgically-minded would be opposed to this adaptation, to this "improvement in living standards." Still, standard of living doesn't equate with quality of life. What conveys this need for quality or, as Hannah Arendt says, this need for the mind to have life?

Very quickly after Marx, it became clear that the "revolution" ("material goods" plus "happiness") wouldn't happen in the most advanced countries. Rosa Luxemburg had already noted that these countries balance their crisis by feeding off the world's misery, and the process hasn't finished, to say the least. Do you make revolution in the poorest countries, among the "weak links," by the pressure of some dictatorial political party that gives birth to totalitarianism? Leninism failed tragically. As tragically as Hitler's madness, when he guaranteed the happiness of the *Volk* by arrogating the right to wipe other people from the surface of the earth, innocent human beings who ceased being such for the Nazis quite simply because they were other, because they were Jewish. Today though, the world's reserve of misery is still too great, intolerably so, but it is diminishing. Especially in the democratic countries of Europe. The people of these countries find themselves at an unprecedented historical crossroads. The French people embody both the discontent of the *misérables* (Robespierre's and Hugo's discontent) and the excess of a nation capable of jouissance (Rabelais to Laclos and

Colette). Is it a handicap? It can be an opportunity, if we don't die off in the meantime, celebrating the end of history in a thousand marketing ploys. Increasingly, on the other hand, the new forms of revolt we mentioned require the intervention of both the elites and certain distinct groupings—the professions, specific age-groups and so on. So perhaps it's impossible to reconcile the "people," "elites" and "opinion sectors." It's difficult certainly, but is it impossible? Take these elites—it's not the people who hold them in low esteem, it's the elites themselves. When they're not being anxiety-struck, they wrap themselves up in their specialized subject instead and tear themselves apart in fratricidal battles. But these elites exist, and as much in the labs as in the universities, in artistic creation too—ambitious cooperation does happen. Take this meeting between the domains of biology, law, philosophy, psychology and aesthetics as an example. This is necessary both to sustain the rise of biology but also to confront its deviancy. It's French researchers who have best figured this out. Public opinion isn't indifferent to this.

So, are we regressing by comparison with the sixties? People say that in relation to the US, nothing is happening anymore in France. That remains to be seen. Apparently, what is happening is less spectacular—the spectacle overshadowed by the "show." More thorough work is rarely or poorly programmed for the small screen, but it's still going on, perhaps more seriously than before...

Deleuze talked about the sadness of generations without master-thinkers. Do you have the impression that the young generations don't have any?

I don't share this nostalgia. I don't really think I need intellectual masters and I don't have the impression that the young people I know are asking for them either. Actually what they need is authority. It's not the same thing. In this so-called new world order of automation, which is simultaneously hyper-complex and indifferent to us, what the individual who feels threatened by "new maladies of the soul" is asking for is to have a genuine experience. And they grant authority to those who convey such experience. A person with experience is rare. What I mean by that is someone who has made their journey to the end of the night, fully aware of the loss of self but who succeeded in regaining his self. What flows from the words he takes from that experience is knowledge. He is neither a guru nor a dry savant, but someone who both knows and is flesh and blood into the bargain. My students follow professors who bring them information, but they respect, and sometimes adore those who enliven their discourse with experience. What they read passionately are far less the technical works that super-achievers devoured during the '70s and '80s, but the Church Fathers, the mystics and the theologians. It's not easy to respond to this demand, this curiosity. We are bidden to participate in a constant, reciprocal transference, which is about going along with it while keeping yourself at a distance. It's about identifying with suffering and trauma, making desire come on its own, letting desire have its experience. Then guiding those who ask you towards a living knowledge grounded on that basis alone, not bringing them to a "dead letter." If you fail, the way is clear for religious or ideological spiritualism, which speculates on this demand for authority and experience. Psychoanalysts and writers, artists and researchers in the human sciences are perhaps more sensitive than others to this situation. But masters in thought, no, what would you do with them? Everyone knows that no-one knows everything, no-one really masters anything...

"If you accept the idea that the temporality of a society organizes itself around the axis of past, present and future, what you see today is a surfeit of the present, to the detriment of the past and the future." Zaki Laïdi writes this in Esprit *(Feb. 1998). Do young people miss the future?*

But we've never talked more about memory! Young people aren't cultivated like some of us were, but let's not forget the demographic flux and social mixing that is hidden by the word "young people." We're endlessly living off of commemorations and other trials of memory, no-one can escape them. Are they assimilated, taken in? We fall back on to the same problem, i.e. the necessity of living out a meaning or a value, desiring them, loving them, hating them, rebelling with them in order to build a psychic life, a form of liberty... As for the future, ideologies that promise you something are bankrupt, and those who regret that can feel bad, it's true. Besides, the new automated world order doesn't grant the possibility of any other future other than adapting to this one. Which means lots of unemployed and other excluded people, we can't repeat that enough. Just one more reason for appreciating the urgency you sense in France. Beyond a case of national depression, it's an appeal for another civilization. Notably, this factors into greater courage in the combat for a social vision for Europe. I think anti-Europeans of every stripe are old-time nationalists who cloak their inability to question their own inertia, idleness and protectionism in populist demagogy. But to harmonize the European union and be receptive to revolt at the same time is something else entirely.

On a more metaphysical level, your question on the future brings us back to the promise and to time, and hence to eschatological and religious problems. It's easy to believe that the religious person is a humble person who leaves it all up to God and his promises of immortality, or at least of a future. But Freud remarked in *Future of an Illusion* that on the contrary, it's the atheist who is resolved to true humility because he admits his limits, what is impossible for him, his mortality or uncertainty at his future. Such humility isn't resignation but on the contrary the true, perhaps only motive that enables you to fight for a future that isn't guaranteed by anyone or for anyone—neither by the family, society, or providence. For that future I can only count on my own energies and those of my accomplices. I don't wait for help, I take things upon myself, and bring people into collusion with me. So the future isn't the expectation of welfare, it's at the horizon of a sort of perpetual renaissance—if we're capable of it.

This renaissance also applies to love. What is difficult to understand with you is the type of place you reserve for men and women in heterosexual couples. I'll make my question more precise. In what you call her "apparent realism," one has the impression that to be autonomous a woman has to live "with the presence of the child and the lover" and under appropriate economic conditions.

I don't understand what you don't understand. In *The Sense and Non-Sense of Revolt* I say that the woman is a stranger to the phallic order she nonetheless adheres to, if only because she is a speaking being, a being of thought and law. But she keeps a distance vis-à-vis the social order, its rules, political contracts, etc., and this makes her skeptical, potentially atheist, ironic and all in all, pragmatic. I'm not really in the loop, says the woman, I'm staying outside, I don't believe in it, but I play the game, and at times, better than others. A sort of imbalance results, giving rise to a feminine melancholia that's both endemic and deep. But, to compensate for this, you also get efforts to "carry on as if." Hence: seduction and make-up, or when it takes a really serious turn, abnegation, overwork, etc. How do you balance out this strangeness, this "eternal irony of the community" old Hegel feared and demeaned? Firstly, by economic independence. A job, work for all women. Psychic and existential reassurance as well: this should be an on-going job because, more than a man, a woman can be inconsolable when in mourning over her mother, a mother she only rarely manages to break off from. Husbands and lovers try to offset the Bovary blues that affect most of us. But it's the child who is the real presence and it becomes her permanent analyst: a relay for narcissism, the ultimate and indispensable other, a sublime creation, even if the child itself is nothing special, something no aesthetic or religious object could ever equal. Above all the child is an other to break away from, it is whom I give to, and who is a gift to me, who continuously reminds me that I am only separation and gift.

Women hold the key to the race. Does that mean that men hold the keys to revolt?

Women hold the key to the species on the condition that they share it with men. At least given the present state of science... let's joke for a moment! But beyond spermatozoa and ova, since they're still indispensable, haven't we sufficiently insisted in our conversation on the fact that a human being, a speaking subject, emerges from a tripartite structure where the father plays an essential role? As for revolt, I'm in the middle of writing a work dedicated to the feminine genius—nothing less than that. It examines women's contribution to the twentieth-century crisis of culture—Hannah Arendt, Melanie Klein and Colette. They are three very different authors, all women of revolt, if you insist on reusing the term. Take Arendt, a philosopher and political thinker, who upsets the university establishment in the US, stays close to Heidegger, but stigmatizes his compromises and above all, displaces his thought in an unprecedented examination of human responsibilities at the heart of politics and modern history. Or Melanie Klein, who insists on psychosis and death drives in a different way from Freud, who thereby makes contemporary psychoanalysis a suitable way of thinking about the traumas of the century. And finally Colette, who accepted institutional honors while remaining insolently sensual, impenitent. No, women have a place in revolt. And I don't understand why you want me to separate men and women so unkindly, like Vigny, and Proust who reused his quotation: "The two sexes will die each on their own." I hope not! The war of the sexes may well have made a lot of victims but we're in this together for better or for worse.

REVOLT AND REVOLUTION

An Interview by Rainer Ganahl

POLITICS AND PSYCHOANALYSIS

Revolt as Retrospective Return □ Searching For Truth □
Rehabilitate Memory □ Revolution, a Betrayal of Revolt □
Psychoanalysis Against Normalization □ Anxiety and Revolt □
Social Bond and Religion: the Oedipal Revolt □ Dogmatism
and Fundamentalism □ Political Movements □ Feminist
Groups □ Leaders and Rulers □ Franz Fanon

What is revolt, and where does this need for revolt come from?

In contemporary society the word revolt means very schematically
political revolution. People tend to think of extreme left movements linked to the Communist revolution or to its leftist
developments. I would like to strip the word "revolt" of its purely political sense. In all Western traditions, revolt is a very deep
movement of discontent, anxiety and anguish. In this sense, to
say that revolt is only politics is a betrayal of this vast movement.
People have reduced, castrated and mutilated the concept of
revolt by turning it only into politics. Therefore if we still want to

conquer new horizons, it is necessary to turn away from this idea and to give the word revolt a meaning that is not just political. I try to interpret this word in a philosophical and etymological sense. The word revolt comes from a Sanskrit root that means to discover, open, but also to turn, to return. This meaning also refers to the revolution of the earth around the sun, for example. It has an astronomical meaning, the eternal return. On a more philosophical level, since Plato, through St. Augustine and until Hegel and Nietzsche, there is a meaning that I wanted to rehabilitate and that you would find equally rehabilitated by Freud and Proust. It is the idea that being is within us and that the truth can be acquired by a retrospective return, by anamnesis, by memory. The return to oneself leads the individual to question his truth, much like what is accomplished with philosophical dialogues, for example Plato's. Something that prayer and all forms of meditation also accomplish according to St. Augustine. I think that Freud gave a new meaning to this retrospective return by asking psychologically troubled patients to search for memories of their traumas and to tell their stories. Why is this both different from the tradition and analogue to it? It is analogue because it is always about searching for the truth through a return to the past in the sense of Plato and St. Augustine. On the other hand it is different because Freud does not think that we can stabilize ourselves in a contemplation of God or Being. Stability is provisional. It is the conflicts that are eternal because there is pleasure in conflict. The individual, in this return to him or herself, experiences division, conflict, pleasure and jouissance in this fragmentation. This is the modern vision of psychic truth. I think that in the automated modern world the depth of psychic life, the liberation of psychic life, the search for truth in the interrogation and the questioning are all aspects that are overlooked. We are expected to be performing entities. At best, we are asked to work well and to buy as much as possible. This whole problematic of interrogation, of the return to the self, the questioning and the conflicts that are sources of human freedom have become obliterated, rejected or even destroyed parameters. The culture that arises from this situation is a culture of entertainment rather than one of interrogation and revolt. I would say it is an essential kind of resistance in a technocratic society to rehabilitate memory along with the questioning and to allow the conflicts of the individual to take place, thus creating a culture that would satisfy these needs.

It's rather paradoxical if you think that today in the "New Technologies" you also encounter an excess of memory.

Yes, but what one calls memory is in fact a storing of information that has nothing to do with interrogation. There is no place for nothingness or for questioning in this storage system, it is merely an accumulation of data, a databank. What Plato and St. Augustine referred to as memory was a permanent doubting. Its essential aspect is nothingness, from Heidegger through Sartre. The question of nothingness is essential as an aspect of freedom. But what is the meaning of nothingness: the possibility to rebel, to change and to transform. With a computer you simply store data as such. But the idea of a transformative creativity that emerges through nothingness and through questioning are parameters that are completely dismissed.

I think that storing information is an ideology in itself.

It is precisely a technocratic ideology that is supposed to abolish anxiety. But what I am saying is the opposite: anxiety, repulsion, nothingness are essential aspects of freedom. That's what revolt is. When one abolishes revolt that is linked to anxiety and rejection, there is no reason to change. You store things and keep storing. It's a banker's idea, not an idea of a rebel, which spreads this technocratic ideology.

In psychoanalysis you take the practice of revolt in the Latin sense of the word revolvere. *However psychoanalysis has been criticized for not taking sociopolitical phenomena which underlie any social upheaval sufficiently into consideration. Could you elaborate on this?*

What I am trying to say is that the meaning of revolt, which could be taken as revolution, would reduce the concept to sociopolitical protests. This constitutes a betrayal of revolt. Very often political movements have tried to abolish old values in order to replace them with new ones, but without questioning these new ideas. For example, the French Revolution was against the Ancien Regime. As a consequence the Third-Estate becomes the new power, however the Third-Estate ceases to question itself. This is why the bourgeois revolution initially turns the rule over to the guillotine, before turning to moral order. Thus, you can see how the French Revolution becomes a betrayal of the initial movement of revolt. If you take the Russian Revolution, things are even clearer. The Russian Revolution established a totalitarian regime which betrayed the revolt, because the rebellion against the old bourgeois world forgot to question the new values that it put in its place.

The so-called proletariat was the bearer of freedom. But the proletariat later became the Communist party without self-questioning, thus killing freedom. When one says that the solution is found in social protest, it demonstrates a limited understanding of things. Social protest should not be a purpose in itself. It should be an integral part of a larger process of general anxiety which is simultaneously psychic, cultural, religious anxiety, etc. Freudianism has no political problems since it is interested above all in the psychic malaise of people. On the other hand it is true that a certain type of psychoanalysis, namely American psychoanalysis, does not see this interrogation as an open process, but as a standardization: "You are a homosexual, I am going to change you into a heterosexual. Let's say you are not successful in your job, the purpose of analysis is to make you a CEO or owner and to earn a lot of money." I am challenging this normative vision of psychoanalysis which constitutes a sort of decline of psychoanalysis. This is why one cannot expect psycho-analysis to solve social problems. On the other hand, one can challenge psychoanalysis when it degenerates into normalization.

In my practice I try to keep social conditions in mind, so that when someone speaks about his or her financial difficulties or political questions I am willing to listen to these questions. But it is also true that it is not the role of psychoanalysis to prepare people for union activism or to become members of political parties, whether left or right. What concerns me essentially is to provoke people's anxieties and to free their creativity. At that point, it is up to them to decide if this creativity will play itself out at a political level, at a union level, at a cultural or sexual level, but again it is not the role of the analyst to train political protesters.

The word "revolution" no longer possesses a lot of value in Western intellectual circles, but it has a violent actuality in "fundamentalist" countries. How do you see the relationship between revolution and revolt? I would like to add a note to what you just said concerning the economy of this word. In a certain way, the word revolt as you

*use it follows the same strategy that one can see in the field of eco-
nomics, which has also vampirized this kind of vocabulary. I do not
want to say that you vampirize it in the same manner, but advertising
agencies do so. They speak for example of the "revolution" of the New
Technologies as a way of selling a product.*

These days, only Le Pen speaks of revolution in France. Likewise,
when I turn the television on, it is the product to clean washing
machines that is revolutionary. To propose a new product against
another is, I think, a purely nihilistic idea. One establishes a value
for an object that goes against previous values and is presented
with this new product as something absolute that will solve all
problems. This same spirit animates Stalinism or fascism: a dogmatism that stops the process of revolt. What I want to rehabilitate
is this idea of revolt as permanent anxiety. Heidegger speaks of
annihilating [anéantir], not of negation in the logical sense of the
term, as part of a process leading to repulsion of negativity and
rejection. This constitutes a fundamental anxiety which is in fact
the foundation of freedom.

*This fundamental anxiety is also produced by the world economic
situation. All social systems that have been instituted are in the
process of being dismantled and destroyed. What exactly does the
practice of provoking people's anxieties...*

There are two things: there is daily anguish because people live in
instability, but we should also mention what is proposed in relation
to that anxiety. The Society of Spectacle tells us not to worry: this
is the revolutionary product, you are going to become a consumer
and arrive at a solution. What I am saying is that one shouldn't
deny the anxiety of the unemployed, the anxiety of the adolescent,

the anxiety of women, which are all integral parts of existence. Our thoughts and culture should accompany this anxiety without resorting to products or solutions like the National Front, which sees itself as the ultimate solution. Then, what kind of thought is it that accompanies anxiety and which is a sort of accompanying catharsis? I see it in certain esthetic works and in some writings like *Finnegans Wake* or in Proust. These are fictions that dig into identities, incessantly asking questions and plunging you into sensations. It's like a kind of language that accompanies this state of anxiety and that allows the individual to remain both anxious and at the same time harmonized, a language which does not reject and exclude him or her. Let's imagine you suffer from anxiety; this is a pathological state. Or you are no longer anxious and you become a consumer, a totally stabilized individual that can be manipulated like a robot. Midway between these two solutions, lie intellectual works and art. These are the actual sites of this anxiety and revolt. The artist's goal is to find the representation of this state of anxiety. It's not a question of claiming that this does not exist or to accept living in marginality, but to represent this revolt in order to survive.

You have commented on revolutionary upheavals in the Arab world. Could you go back to that?

One has often said that religions express a need for purity. This is partly true. For example, all ethnic purifications have adopted the form of a kind of fundamentalism. The Moslem Bosnians do not want to mix with orthodox Serbs and orthodox Serbs have excluded the Bosnians. There is a sort of desire for a pure identity, each clan outbidding the other. This is an aspect of religious fundamentalism. But the other aspect that has been greatly overlooked is that within these movements there is also a movement of rejection and of protest. People who adhere to fundamentalist Islam are rebels against colonialism or against the misery of the Arab world, against Zionist imperialism, against rich, colonial France, against banks, or against a consumer society. This movement of revolt is an essential movement in the religious act. When Freud conceived the constitution of the social contract, he imagined the brothers of the primitive horde killing their father, who represented the law. If you really think about this you can interpret this as a sort of revolt of the young against the old tyrant. Freud refers to this concept as "oedipal revolt." This represents simultaneously both the social bond and religion. Tyranny becomes authority. The brothers who take the place of the father share the women, establish a pact between them, thus giving birth to ceremony; society and religion are born in turn. Therefore there is an element of revolt in the religious act. The issue here is how to take into account the movement of revolt and not let it be strangled by dogmatism. For example all these young people in French suburbs [France-born Algerians] have a need to express their unhappiness. But if you allow this unhappiness to enter Islam, people begin adhering to dogmas. An open mind, a mind set on revolt as I understand it, could become a permanent voice on a level of esthetics, literary creation, discussions, art and the communication which has to be established with these young people. It is this type of liberated form of representation of revolt that I am looking for. This implies that a new cultural space will open up that will not become a space for religious dogma, but one that understands the spiritual anxiety driving religious dogma. In this scenario it is via education, culture and creativity that this need for revolt could be expressed, without strangling itself in dogmatism and fundamentalism.

*Repression against some groups is also real, and revolt has to be orga-
nized in a certain manner in order to conform to specific ideological
movement and politics, as was the case in the decolonization process.
Therefore it is preferable not to revolt through chaotic or individual
acts, but rather through coordinated actions.*

These coordinated acts often turn into fundamentalist sects
because the initial movement consists of opposing the oppressor.
However, they are impervious to the oppression that they themselves create. For example, when Islamic groups oppose colonialists,
one can easily sympathize and understand them. But when they
dismiss women or kill whites, Jews, French or others who do not
adhere to their ideology, you realize that their revolt does not
question itself. These groups do not question their own ideology.
In European left-wing movements this idea of permanent interrogation has been very important. For example, the Trotskyists
against Stalinists. While the Stalinists were fixed in an apparatus,
Trotskyists constantly demanded their apparatus to be questioned. This was undoubtedly a utopian project because there
were also Trotskyist groups that became dogmatic.

When one is involved in politics it is very difficult to escape
dogmatism. The entire history of political movements proves that
they are permeable to dogmatism. One wonders if the realization
of the revolt I am referring to is possible only in the private
sphere: for example, in the psychoanalytical self-interrogation
that people practice with themselves, or in an esthetic framework
(in literary or pictorial creation), or maybe in certain contexts
that are not directly political, but at the meeting point between
different religiosities that question the sacred. I am increasingly
skeptical about the capacity of political movements to remain
places of freedom. Liberation movements are often threatened

and monitored. They become paranoid and turn into sects driven by death and dogmatism, often even with the best intentions. We saw this with the feminist movement which rapidly became a movement of chiefs where women crushed women inside the same group. The strategies of the oppressors against which women fought were reproduced in their own groups.

Were you personally involved in political groups during the sixties?

In fact, I was involved with feminist groups. I will always remember I was given money to go to China to work on a book on Chinese women, and when I finished the book there was a Stalinist-type discussion going on because a couple of women had seized power in the group and reproached me for signing the book in my name. Finally I understood that what they wanted me to do was not to sign it at all, that it should be signed by the head of the group. This was a way of dispossessing the individual in the name of the power that took over the group. Many women less independent than myself suffered from these pressures and became in a way reduced to slavery because a new power had been created within these groups. Let's not even mention sexual abuse, economic abuse, etc. At the time, in the feminist movement an ideology of sect and oppression of individuals emerged. It has been brought to my attention that the same thing happened within movements of the extreme left.

Only in the extreme left?

In extreme right wing movements, it was even worse.

I find that it is important to be skeptical towards institutions. But can you imagine politics or social organizations without institutions?

No, and this is why I cannot see how political groups can escape this. I am, as most French are, very skeptical regarding political life. It is a stopgap. One tries to choose the least dogmatic and corrupt government possible. Often there are attempts to create so-called civil societies based on alternate relationships between groups of young people, women and ecologists. These remain open groups where freedom is possible. Why does this total liberty of which I am speaking remain utopian? Because in the social field we always need a power. Let's imagine you are a group of three people. You need a leader. Or let's say you are in a class. You need a teacher. The issue of power and authority is indispensable. You need to consider the locus of authority which is referred to in psychoanalysis as the "paternal function." But one needs to be able to live with the power of a boss, a politician, and at the same time question their actions. This is very difficult to imagine. Which political party lets itself be interrogated? Which political leader allows himself to be questioned? The need of liberated peoples, who by the way are increasingly made up of Western peoples, is going in this direction. Although we need power, this need to revolt against the authorities is permanent. It is necessary to have alternation, bipartism and far more frequent elections in order to allow political life to breathe. And at the same time we need to create parallel spaces. Aside from political life, we need others spaces, new forms of spirituality where people can attempt to find this kind of freedom that politics cannot provide.

Your individualistic position can be practiced only in an environment that already guarantees a certain degree of freedom.

In Rwanda or in Zaire, this is not possible. At this point they are not free. They need to be framed and assisted. They are only ruled by humanitarian assistance. This is an altogether different experience. They will have our problems once their economic problems are solved.

There is someone who you don't mention in your book and who I find extremely important: Frantz Fanon, a revolutionary and a psychoanalyst that has written the article "On Violence."

I have often heard people speak of him, but I have never read anything by him. He isn't part of the mainstream of Psychoanalytic Studies.

THE SACRED

Women and the Sacred □ The Virgin Mary □ Ideologies and the Sacred □ Sacred and Sense □ Only Individual Revolt Exists □ A Downhill Period □ Consumers and the Elite □ Death of the Intellectuals? □ Adorno and Negativity □ Thinking as Revelation □ Psychosis and Autism □ Art as Experimental Psychosis

You seem to be increasingly interested in new forms of sacredness that would be neither institutional not capitalized by religion in the traditional sense of the term. What is sacredness? How could it be separated from religion? The relationship of religions with sacredness is often repressive: one doesn't need to asks question, but rather to believe.

It is about recognizing fundamental values and how we can continue to question them. This is why I said these new forms of sacredness should not run aground in a cult. What is sacred for people today? What does it mean for women, children and different classes in society? What is its relationship to life, to survival, to life and death? We must reflect upon these essential challenges with one's religious inheritance: Judaism, Christianity, Buddhism and maybe also with new ways of thinking as we have learned them from psychoanalysis and contemporary art. Forms of sacredness that are different and open. I am in the process of writing a book together with Catherine Clement on *Women and the sacred*. We raise questions concerning the relationship women have had with sacredness in the history of religion, the difficulties women have faced with religious institutions, etc. In the book we ask what is considered sacred by today's woman: the right to life, the right over her body, the right of abortion and contraception, but also the right to become a mother. Without being either the Virgin Mary or a prostitute, what is the profile of the woman that comes out of this? The evolution of the clichés that we have experienced until now continues to evolve, both the sacred side and the blasphemous one, for which the exact forms have not yet been determined. I do not want to propose a form. I believe we have to encourage these interrogations without being nihilistic and declaring that there is nothing sacred.

Do you believe that it is more productive to reuse a metaphysical concept with such a repressive and problematical history?

Yes, I believe that it is more productive because it replaces the word "sense." For a lot of people of my generation the term is often debased, rendered too banal and considered outright insufficient. I prefer to employ the word sacredness. Meaning is produced by the word sacredness. There is a swarm of people disillusioned by ideologies that turn to sacred, traditional values. Despite this, I understand the importance of values, but it would be necessary for these values to be questioned.

Do you believe more in the use of the irrational and non-discursive concept of the sacred than in the use of another term? Even the word creativity has been completely deformed.

You have the right to your creativity in a ghetto, and nobody is interested in that.

Globalization and the interconnection of the world, organized by hyper-powerful networks and markets, are also factors that render any revolt difficult, if not futile. How do you see the structures of subjectivity change in this "new world order"?

It is true that everything moves from system to system. But one cannot revolt against systems. I think that the possibility for individual revolt still exists. This could appear as too minimal, but I think that it is the only possibility that remains: individual interrogation. This does not necessarily mean egoism. It means placing a greater demand on oneself, and treating others with more generosity. Indeed, I think that the only space of honesty possible is the individual space.

How can one guarantee this sort of freedom? For example, advertising and commercial language is a language that sells so-called "personality" and "creativity."

It is going to be very difficult to remain one of the last members of an elite. We are in a period that resembles somewhat the end of the Roman Empire, where the utopia according to which the whole world would be capable of self-interrogation, of self-questioning and of a free life, is in the process of disappearing. We will increasingly become roboticized masses and consumers. There will be few people left who keep a memory of the past and who question this past. They will form an elite like the clerics of the Middle Ages. Maybe we are living through a downhill period...

What surprises me in your text is that you explain Sartre, Aragon and Barthes to students and readers as if they were part of history. You seem to imply that the current generation can no longer produce intellectuals. Is the issue of the possibility of revolt related in turn to the possibility of the existence of intellectuals?

Are intellectuals dead today? I hope not since I am here. But there are just a few of us.

You have spoken a lot about negativity, which is central to Adorno's thinking. In France, Adorno has not been read extensively.

It is a type of German thinking I like a lot. But it is Hegel, and particularly the role he assigned to negativity, that has been emphasized in German philosophy. It is a fundamental aspect and today many sociologists refuse it. They tend to think of society as a calculation, as a program, as a storage site of information. I heard sociologist Alain Touraine say that this philosophy, the negative, was old. I think this is wrong; without negativity, there is no longer freedom or thinking. One must consider thinking as a revelation, an exploration, an opening, a place of freedom. If this aspect of the negative were eliminated, it would lead straight into the robotization of humanity. I am frightened by this prospect. My interest in Hannah Arendt is also related to this idea in that she tried to rehabilitate anxious thinking [*la pensée inquiète*] against calculated thinking that is just "computerizing."

You attribute a specific role to the arts and particularly to contemporary art. You write that the privilege of contemporary art is to accompany us in the "new diseases of the soul": psychosis and autism. Could you specify the relationship between the arts, psychosis and autism?

Psychosis is a destruction of the symbolic, something able to drive us into delirious states, violence and turmoil of thinking. Autism is the impossibility to access language. It manifests itself essentially in the child that is invaded by sensation [*sensorialité*] but that cannot access signs and language. I often have the impression that works of art are psychoses, experimental autism probably with an autistic and psychotic latency. But at the same time artists rely on language and carry out social activities. They are not in asylums but participate in social functions in a manner more or less normative. With increased negativity, they produce experimental psychoses or experimental autism and drive us to the limits of our identities. If you see a "dripping" of Pollock or an installation in which there are disparate objects, you are driven into twilight states of mind. It is evident that these are forms of regression that are requested. Why is this profitable? Because we have a representation of these states of malaise which we experience individually and that render us extremely morbid. Through contemporary art we feel a recognition, a division of these states and these new forms of sacredness.

Concerning the subtitle of your book The Sense and Non-Sense of Revolt, *what are the "powers and limits of Psychoanalysis" today?*

The "powers" reside in the ability to demand interrogation. "Limits" could be thought of as meaning that one cannot do much more than give people free rein with their political and esthetic creativity; and not providing responses to these questions. Once you are under interrogation, it's your turn to play. In that, psychoanalysis can help leading you to anamnesis and to interrogation.

CAN THERE BE REVOLT WITHOUT REPRESENTATION?

An Interview by Rubén Gallo

POWERS OF REVOLT

Revolt as a Dialectical Process □ Psychic Revolt, Analytical Revolt, Artistic Revolt Are a Permanent Questioning □ Oedipus Complex Is About Desire and Death □ The Complexities of Representation □ The "Right" Kind of Violence □ Renewal and Regeneration

In The Sense and Non-Sense of Revolt *(1996) you explore the notion of revolt, an experience of questioning and transgression that serves to renew and sustain the life of the psyche. Your book presents a genealogy of revolt that extends from the archaic rebellion of the brothers in Freud's* Totem and Taboo *to twentieth-century experiences that include psychoanalysis as well as the works of Louis Aragon, Jean-Paul Sartre, and Roland Barthes.*

Most of your examples involve a form of representation—art, literature, the construction of a personal narrative in psychoanalysis. Do you think that revolt can occur outside of representation? Can there be an unmediated, unrepresented experience of revolt?

I see revolt as a dialectical process, and I think that an act of rebellion always involves representation. Today the word "revolt" has become assimilated to Revolution, to political action. The events of the Twentieth Century, however, have shown us that political "revolts"—Revolutions—ultimately betrayed revolt, especially the psychic sense of the term. Why? Because revolt, as I understand it—psychic revolt, analytic revolt, artistic revolt—refers to a state of permanent questioning, of transformation, change, an endless probing of appearances. The history of political revolts shows that the process of questioning has ceased. Once in power the French Revolution ceased to call into question its own values. The Russian Revolution stopped questioning its own ideals and degenerated into totalitarianism. In light of the betrayal of revolt in Revolution, I wanted to rehabilitate the microscopic sense of the word, its etymological and literary sense in which the root "vel" means unveiling, returning, discovering, starting over. This is the permanent questioning that characterizes psychic life and, at least in the best of cases, art.

It is this sense of permanent questioning that Freud sought to rehabilitate when he used the term "revolt" to describe the Oedipus complex. In the myth, Oedipus interrogates the Sphinx, he asks questions, he wants to know. What does he want to know? He wants to know the potential of desire and death, two of the great themes that structure human experience. For Freud—and we have often misunderstood him on this point—the essence of the Œdipus complex, the source of the subject's autonomy, is not about imposing norms or laws, but about questioning desire and death through a continuous process of self-examination. If we understand the analytic adventure through this act of questioning, we can arrive at a freer and more open conception of psychoanalysis than the one assigned to normative therapy. This act of questioning is also present in artistic experience, in the rejection and renewal of old codes of representation staged in painting, music, or poetry.

In other words, the act of representation is an act of revolt. Some forms of representation, however, contain more explicit references to experiences of revolt than others. Many artists, for example, have attempted to represent violence, to translate their experience of an extreme form of revolt—death and destruction—into a work of art.

I have found that representations of violence tend to employ one of two opposing strategies: either a literal *strategy that reproduces the experience of violence as faithfully as possible—for example certain early works by Vito Acconci, or the photos of death and genocide collected in the "Polysexuality" issue of* Semiotext(e)—or a metaphorical *strategy that renounces direct reference in favor of suggestion and evocation, as in the case of Alfredo Jaar's* Real Pictures, *an installation about the Rwandan genocide in which photographs of the massacre were encased in black boxes and could not be seen. In your opinion, which of these two strategies for representing violence constitutes a more successful act of revolt? What effects do these two forms of representation produce in the viewer's psyche?*

I will answer by invoking a more archaic example, one that illustrates the complexities of representation. I am thinking of the representation of violence in Picasso's work, especially in *Les Demoiselles d'Avignon* and *Guernica*. The first of these paintings depicts a group of prostitutes; the other, the bombardment of a Spanish town during the Civil War. Both works transpose the violence of their subject-matter into the field of representation, exerting violence against previous artistic forms and demolishing traditional pictorial codes. *Les Demoiselles d'Avignon* is not a mere photographic depiction of prostitution, and *Guernica* is not a simple documentary about the Spanish Civil War. On the contrary, these paintings enact very violent transformations of the codes of representation.

What matters most in these works is, on the one hand, the adaptation to the "external world"—I put this term in quotes because this exteriority can never exist on its own—and, on the other, the creative act of producing meaning, an act that is ultimately contingent on that presumed exteriority. In his work, the artist performs the "right" kind of violence: by appropriating what lies outside him, he achieves a balance between the self and the world. This very delicate alchemy, whose value we often underestimate, is an act of creation that takes place precisely at this interstice between the individual and the world—a privileged space where metaphor, metonymy, and other rhetorical figures come into play. The artist's role is not to make a faithful copy of reality, but to shape our attitude towards reality. This balance, this harmony, this genuine act of revolt is not about domination or concealment, but about the interstice, about appropriating and being possessed, about the resonance between the self and the world.

So representation is an inherently violent act, even if it does not refer literally or metaphorically to actual events like murder or massacre. Perhaps Lautréamont came to a similar conclusion when he described Shakespeare's poetry as an intensely violent affair: "Chaque fois que j'ai lu Shakespeare, il m'a semblé que je déchiquète la cervelle d'un jaguar"—*Everytime I read Shakespeare I feel like I'm tearing apart the brain of a jaguar.*

Exactly. Lautréamont experiences this intensity when he *reads* Shakespeare, an act of appropriation that exposes the violence in Shakespeare's language as well the violence in the act of reading.

Could we then say that every act of representation entails experience of violence? Could we see literature, art, and psychoanalysis not only as experiences of revolt but also as experiences of psychic violence?

I would not use the word "violence" because it can be misleading. In revolt there is violence, there is destruction, but there are also many other elements. I like the term revolt because of its etymological association with return, patience, distance, repetition, elaboration. Revolt is not simply about rejection and destruction; it is also about starting over. Unlike the word "violence," "revolt" foregrounds an element of renewal and regeneration.

LIMITS OF REBELLION

Positive and Destructive Revolt □ Acting-Out □ Freud and Deleuze on Sado-Masochism □ The Paternal Function □ The New Maladies of the Soul □ *Totem and Taboo* □ No Revolt Without Authority □ The Social Contract □ Regression into Barbarism □ Killing and Slandering □ Civilization on the Brink of Collapse □ Delirium □ Proust Polymorphous □ Hannah Arendt's *Life of the Mind* □ Decapitation □ Women's Suffering □ Representation of Pain.

The subtitle of your book The Sense and Non-Sense of Revolt *is "The powers and limits of psychoanalysis." So far, we have discussed the powers of revolt—its expression in art, its powers of regeneration for psychic space, its assertion of individuality and creation—and I would now like to turn our discussion to the limits of this act. An individual can rebel against norms, against interdictions, against society, but if this rebellion surpasses certain limits, it becomes "acting-out" and can lead to violence, destruction, even murder. What are the differences between the positive aspect of revolt that you explore in*

*your book and the destructive revolt that would lead to various forms
of acting-out? What is the boundary between the two?*

Acting-out does not go via representation. Acting-out is a
destruction without signs, an act excluded from time and
return, from appeasement and distance. Acting-out is a pure
explosion of drives, as we see in its extreme forms, like murder
and suicide. A representation, on the other hand—a painting by
de Kooning, for example—distances itself from violence
through the appropriation of old artistic forms and the invention of new ones. Art possesses a cyclical quality that inscribes
experience in time, perhaps because the act of creation uses
signs and not external objects.

*What is the source of acting-out, of behavior that can lead to van-
dalism or aggression against others? In the history of psychoanalysis,
I have found two contradictory explanations of these extreme forms
of violence: the first is Freud's theory of sadomasochism, which sees
sadism—aggression—as the outcome of instincts that have not been
sufficiently repressed or sublimated. Violent behavior would arise
from an individual who has been insufficiently socialized, insufficiently subjected to the law. Closer to our time, Gilles Deleuze, in
his Introduction to Sacher-Masoch's* Venus in Furs, *claims that the
sadist internalizes social laws and interdictions to such an extreme
degree that he becomes all superego and must find an ego to subju-
gate in other people. Violent behavior would occur in individuals
who have been socialized too well, because sadism stems from the
law and not from instincts. Which side of this debate would you
support? Does violent behavior stem from rampant instincts or
from an inflated superego?*

Freud never saw sadism as a mere explosion of drives. In *Totem and Taboo*, he relates his theory of drives to the "paternal function," and thus the notion of the superego is bound to the theory of sadism presented in the *Metapsychological Papers*. We have to read Freud attentively. He constructed his theories in stages, and thus certain texts emphasize certain notions, like the drives, while other texts might insist on other aspects, like the paternal function or the superego. Concepts are not always grouped together, and we should read Freudian texts through time, constructing a reading *based on* Freud rather than theorizing *through* him.

Freudians consider sadism as inseparable from the violence of the superego. Lacan used to say "*C'est le surmoi qui dit jouit!*" — it is the superego's injunction that demands *jouissance* and controls the drives. Unlike animals, human beings do not have access to unrestrained, untamed drives. Human drives are always linked to prohibitions, to an internalization of interdictions in the form of a superego. It is *against* this prohibition that the drive acts. I think that Freud always insisted on the force of *both* prohibitions and drives.

Clearly, sadism could never develop in a person born with weak drives, but neither could it develop in someone lacking a strong superego. In Freudian theory there is a dialectic between the force of the drive and the force of the superego. The two always go together.

As a practicing psychoanalyst, you must often encounter patients who act-out, not by vandalizing or killing, but simply by inflicting violence onto their psyche in the form of neurotic or obsessional behavior. Could we explain these pathologies through the theories of sadism presented by Freud and Deleuze? Do they stem from a deficient superego that has become either too weak or too powerful?

I have found that many of my patients suffer from new configurations of pathologies that I call "the new maladies of the soul." Many of them experience a drop in their powers of representation, a deterioration of their psychic apparatus. Their superego was not internalized properly, and the drives, even if weak, run wild. At this point, these passions can degenerate into acting out, somatization, or drug addictions. These are actions that are not represented, that are not subjected to the laws of the superego, or even to the subtle norms of artistic representation. Today, these new maladies, these acts of destruction, pose the greatest and most disturbing threat to psychic space.

You come to a similar conclusion about the importance of authority in Le Sens et non-sens de la révolte. *Your analysis of Freud's* Totem and Taboo *focuses not only on the act of rebellion against the father, but also comments extensively on paternal authority. In Freud's myth the father represents two types of authority: he is a totalitarian ruler, but he also embodies the authority that holds together this primitive community. The brothers rebel against the father's authoritative rule, yet by becoming the new rulers they come to identify with—and incorporate—his benevolent authority.* "Homo sapiens *becomes a social animal by identifying not with the tyranny that oppressed him but with the function of paternal authority."*

Using the brothers' archaic rebellion as an example, you claim that authority and revolt are caught in a dialectic. There can be no revolt without authority, because the individual rebels precisely in order to occupy the position of authority. Thus, you point out that today "one of the reasons for our inability to stage a symbolic revolt is perhaps the fact that authority, values, and the law have become inconsistent and empty forms." *The lack of a benevolent paternal authority has led to a crisis of symbolic revolt.*

Today, however, there are still many societies around the globe ruled by totalitarian systems, both on the left and on the right. Can revolt occur under these circumstances? Is there a point at which authority becomes too powerful and destroys the possibility of revolt?

In *Totem and Taboo*, Freud describes how tyranny is transformed into authority through revolt. The story begins with a despotic father who rules over a group of brothers, denying them access to the women he keeps. Overcome by jealousy, the brothers rebel, they act out and kill the father. Their next step is to transform tyranny into authority: they ingest the father's body, they incorporate him and assume his role in the society, thereby establishing a pact. This is the origin of the social contract, a set of symbolic laws that represent authority. Where there was murder there will now be a set of rules: rules governing the exchange of women, alimentary or moral prohibitions, and so on. Tyranny and execution are transformed into a set of symbolic norms that constitute the basis of morality, religion, and ultimately, civilization.

Today, the state of the world poses a crucial question: Are we still living in a civilization structured by authority and symbolic laws, or—like the patients suffering from the "new maladies of the soul"—have we lost our capacity to represent, to maintain a superego and a paternal function? And if so, are we not threatened with a regression into barbarism, into tyranny? We have seen it happen in totalitarianism, in Nazism and Stalinism. Hanna Arendt said that the Twentieth Century has witnessed the abolition of two great prohibitions, of two forms of the superego. The Nazis abolished the injunction against murder (given in the commandment "Thou shalt not kill") and the Stalinists did away with the prohibition against slandering ("Thou shalt not bear false testimony against your neighbor"). Stalinism, in its incitement of slanderous accusations, repudiated the principle of respect for the other.

We should ask if today, in our democracies, we are not in danger of sliding into a "soft" type of totalitarianism in which moral prohibitions—the norms established by the primeval brothers in their pact—are being eroded along with the capacity to represent. Without restraint, without the internalization of a superego or an ideal ego, there can be no values, no meaning, no representation; everything is allowed, including suicide, somatization, acting-out, vandalism, and even murder. We live in a time in which civilization is on the brink of collapse. Fortunately I am referring only to extreme cases, but there are certain fringes of society where this danger is imminent.

Would you consider the weakening of this benevolent authority, of the laws and interdictions that constitute the basis of society, as one of the causes for the recent proliferation of mass suicides linked to religious cults? In these extreme forms of acting-out we can sometimes recognize a desperate attempt to invent some sort of higher authority—a despotic authority that demands sacrifices and human lives.

There are many signs of this collapse of the symbolic function: mass suicide, drug addiction, unemployment, social marginalization, as well as the empire of images and the destruction of the family. A function that human beings fostered during thousands of years, the internalization of prohibitions in the form of a superego or an ideal ego, is being destroyed, and psychic space is adrift, lost in a state of delirium.

I can think of another reason for the proliferation of these cults, which promise a reassuring sense of belonging: the loss of identity in our societies. You once wrote that it is one of the most common afflictions that you find in your patients: a feeling of not belonging anywhere, of being alienated from the world.

Loss of identity, however, is not always a pathology; it also occurs in the extreme states that push our subjectivity to the limits, like love or jouissance. You have portrayed Proust as lacking a clearly recognizable identity: he did not belong to any one group, he was not part of the homosexual community, of a specific literary circle, or even of a social class. Yet Proust's attempt to translate this feeling of "not belonging" into words was intensely productive. Ultimately it yielded the masterpiece À la Recherche du temps perdu. *What, then, is the difference between these two forms of identity loss—the pathological experience and the creative?*

This is a very good question, although I do not agree entirely with your account of Proust. Proust, on the contrary, belongs everywhere. He belongs to a plurality, to a multiplicity. The role of the writer is precisely to complicate the notion of belonging: one has to belong and not belong. Proust is *and* is not a homosexual. He is in the salons but he is also excluded from them. He is in Madame Verdurin's circle, but he is also outside. Proust is always inside and outside, always on the border. Proust has all the identities in the world, and his identity is always polyphonous and extremely malleable, which is very different from saying that he has no identity. Proust enjoys a polyvalence of experiences that renders him polymorphic, even perverse, in the positive sense of the term. This experiential multiplicity is entirely different from the emptiness and destruction experienced in the loss of identity.

In your recent intellectual biography of Hannah Arendt, you showed her emerging from the destruction and genocide and calling for forgiveness and understanding. You have hailed her as a figure whose experience is marked by the primacy of the life drive. Experience of destruction and loss usually leads to melancholia and depression. What do you think allowed her to transform them into the "life force" that we find in her writing?

I have no idea. All I can do is suggest a few hypotheses. Hannah Arendt's biographer tells us that from the moment she was born, she had a zest for life and an astonishing intellectual curiosity. From very early on she she managed to make of this symbolic dimension the object of her desire—an intense desire for words, for learning and philosophy. A passion that eventually led her to Heidegger.

During her involvement with Heidegger, she was fascinated by the magic of words, the fireworks of ideas, the poetic incantation of Heidegger's thought. She was not blind to his involvement with Nazism, but she was still drawn to the extreme vitality of his words and his mind. She retained her passion for ideas until the end of her life, when she returned to Plato, Saint Augustine, and Kant in the two volumes of *The Life of the Mind*. If we read this work, we can feel her trembling, her intense *jouissance* for language and signification—that extraordinary dimension of human life that Merleau-Ponty once called "an excess on the natural existence of man."

Freud mistakenly believed that women have no relation to the superego or to the ideal-ego. I find it extraordinary that a woman would demonstrate such an intense adherence to the symbolic function, that she would choose her object of desire in this dimension of human experience.

The opening scene of Possession *(1996), your most recent novel, focuses on the decapitated body of a woman found in a park. Decapitation is also the central theme of* Visions capitales *[Capital Visions] an exhibition that you curated in 1998 for the Musée du Louvre. What interests you in decapitation?*

For now I will mention two reasons. First of all, I find decapitation an extremely provoking theme, a classical image that evokes the suffering of women today. After feminism and women's liberation, there is still a great misunderstanding and rejection of feminine experiences, of motherhood, intellectual life, and love, so I wanted to find a disturbing image that would draw attention to this suffering. There is a second reason for this choice: the history of painting contains countless depictions of disembodied heads—think of the head of Christ, for example. This phenomenon, which at first might appear as a simple transposition of castration—the head has been cut off instead of the genitals—has a much deeper significance: it shows us how the very possibility of figuring the human body is inevitably tied to the representation of pain. I found it crucial to highlight this copresence of pain and representation, especially today, when facing pain has become increasingly difficult; pain is either repressed or exploded into violence and massacre. Representation depends on a more intimate experience of pain, an intimacy that is currently in need of renewal.

NOTES

1. Alexandre Kojève (1902-68) conducted the famous seminar on the *Phenomenology of the Mind*, from 1933 to 1936 at the Ecole Pratique des Hautes Etudes; among the audience were Jacques Lacan, Georges Bataille, Maurice Merleau-Ponty and André Breton. Kojève's *Introduction à la lecture de Hegel* (1947), largely based on a re-evaluation of the Master-Slave relationship, heavily influenced the revival of Hegel in France.

2. Edgar Morin (b. 1921). In the late 1950s and early '60s he directed *Arguments*, a Marxist, but non-Stalinist journal influenced by Existentialism. Morin then took up an academic career in sociology, and has produced important works, notably on the sociology of culture and communication.

3. Michel de Certeau (1925-86). In the 1950s, de Certeau, a jesuit, was a scholar of the Christian mystics; his essays on May '68, written between May and September 1968, and published in the journal *Etudes*, nevertheless share a common concern with his earlier work: Certeau focuses on the possibilities of communication, the potential "ways of speaking" of politically or ecclesiastically marginalized groups. Later works include *La Culture au Pluriel* (tr. Culture in the Plural), *La Fable mystique* (tr. The Mystic Fable) and *L'Invention du quotidien* (tr. The Practice of Everyday Life).

4. Georges Canguilhem (1904-95). Historian and philosopher of science. He elaborated a notion of "scientific ideology" in such works as *Le Normal et le pathologique* (1966, tr. The Normal and the Pathological). As in Foucault's work, the emphasis here is on a history of concepts, rather than history-writing in a more traditional sense.

5. *Tel Quel*, an avant-garde journal. From 1960-82 it published important contributions from, among others, Barthes, Derrida, Foucault, Bataille and Sollers which initiated Structuralism and Post-Structuralism in France.

6. Jacques Lacan (1901-1981). Psychiatrist and psychoanalyst known for having rewritten Freud's unconscious in light of Saussurian linguistics. Contrary to most psychoanalysts he insisted that language structures the human subject, rather than the other way round. His assertion that woman is an unknowable, indefinable other has been the chief stimulus to countervailing feminist descriptions of a feminine identity.

7. Roland Barthes (1915-1980). Semiologist and literary theorist, who was seminal in the development of structuralism along linguistic lines. By the late 1960s Barthes had moved away from the "scientific" bent of linguistic theory and devised a more personal approach to literature. The influence of Derrida, Lacan and Kristeva are evident in his work of the 1970s, especially in *Le Plaisir du Texte* (tr. The Pleasure of the Text), which links the practice of reading, writing and text to psychoanalytically-inspired notions of pleasure and jouissance.

8. Claude Lévi-Strauss (b. 1908) Structural anthropologist. His *Tristes Tropiques* (1955) was receptive to the influences of Marxism and psychoanalysis, and reciprocally, the four-volume study of the logic of myths, *Mythologiques* (1964-1971), influenced neighboring intellectual disciplines, such as aesthetics, literary theory and psychoanalysis.

9. Louis Althusser (1928-1990). Marxist philosopher whose works in the 1960s offered influential and original interpretations of Marx (*Pour Marx* [tr. For Marx] appeared in 1965), based on a description of the "structural" relations between economic, political, ideological and theoretical practices; criticism of his positions led him to define Marxist philosophy as a revolutionary weapon rather than as a theory of social practice.

10. "The Enraged." The agitation that sparked off "May '68" began at the University of Paris' campus in the suburbs at Nanterre. What was initially a small group swelled to form a much larger crowd—the *enragés*, as they described themselves—(a reference to the angry crowd unleashed by the French Revolution) after a struggle with the police in the Sorbonne in January 1968.

11. *Rouge* magazine is the weekly newspaper of the LCR, the Ligue communiste révolutionnaire (Revolutionary Communist League), which is Trotskyist in orientation. Daniel Bensaïd, a philosopher at the University of Paris-VIII, has published widely on Marxism and the theory of revolution. On May '68 specifically, see Bensaïd and H. Weber, *Mai 1968, une répétition générale*, Paris, Maspéro, 1968.

12. The Paris Commune of 1871 took its name from the Commune de Paris that was formed in 1789 after the storming of the Bastille. The insurrection of 1871 was led by the largely proletarian parisian electorate against the bourgeois government of Thiers which they accused of having too hastily surrendered to the Prussians. Paris, besieged, survived until May when French troops entered the city. They savagely crushed the revolt in a week that became known as "la semaine sanglante" (the bloody week).

13. Philippe Sollers (b. 1936). Co-founder of *Tel Quel*, and by the 1960s an established young writer celebrated both by Louis Aragon and François Mauriac. Sollers married Julia Kristeva in 1967 and both turned to Marxism and Maoism in the late 60s and 70s. Subsequently his interests became more versatile and ranged from the Bible, America, Catholicism to libertinism.

14. Guy Debord's *La Société du Spectacle*, which appeared in 1967, attacked the modern culture industry as an entity thriving on the ideological illusions of the "spectacle"; in May '68, it seemed that Debord's "Situationist" strategies for reclaiming political and artistic expression from the society of the spectacle were being put in to practice by the *enragés*. See also *Enragés et Situationnistes dans le Mouvement des Occupations* (tr. Enragés and Situationists in the Occupations Movement, France, May 1968) by René Viénet.

15. The *a* stands for *autre* (i.e. other), and is to be distinguished from Autre, the capitalized Other. The concept evolves from a discussion of the Freudian object, but the terminological and conceptual discriminations are specific to Jacques Lacan. For Lacan the subject is constituted in relation to an unknowable Other, an elusive Object. Deprived of such an absolute identification, the subject negotiates a more fluid set of relations to other objects, other alterities that are best designated as *autre, little a.*

16. Gilles Deleuze (1925-1995). A philosopher whose "apprenticeship" in the 1950s and 1960s focused on major thinkers—Nietzsche, Kant, Spinoza, which he turned against Hegelian dialectics. In *Anti-Oedipus* (1972) and *A Thousand Plateaux* (1980) Deleuze collaborated with Felix Guattari and rejected the Oedipus complex, which they consider a scenario bespeaking fixity and repression. It is rejected in favor of the liberating flow of desire.

17. Lionel Jospin became Socialist Prime Minister of France in 1997, and is currently in his second term. He succeeded Alain Juppé who came under investigation for charges of financial irregularities. Jospin has a reputation for probity and personal integrity.

18. Charles Fourier (1772-1837). Fourier's eccentric Utopianism is reflected in a series of works, e.g. *La Théorie des quatre mouvements* (1808, tr. The Theory of the Four Movements), that elaborate a vision of a harmonious society based, notably, on an enhanced appreciation of the (13) passions. The links Fourier elaborated between sexuality and life in society (especially in the *Nouveau Monde amoureux*, only published in 1967), prompted renewed interest in Fourier. Cf. Roland Barthes's essay on *Sade, Fourier, Loyola* (1971).

SEMIOTEXT(E) · NATIVE AGENTS SERIES
Chris Kraus, *Editor*

Airless Spaces Shulamith Firestone

Aliens & Anorexia Chris Kraus

Hannibal Lecter, My Father Kathy Acker

How I Became One of the Invisible David Rattray

If You're a Girl Anne Rower

I Love Dick Chris Kraus

Indivisible Fanny Howe

Leash Jane DeLynn

The Madame Realism Complex Lynne Tillman

The New Fuck You: Adventures In Lesbian Reading Eileen
    Myles & Liz Kotz, eds

Not Me Eileen Myles

The Origin of *the* Species Barbara Barg

The Pain Journal Bob Flanagan

The Passionate Mistakes and Intricate Corruption of One Girl
    in America Michelle Tea

Reading Brooke Shields: The Garden of Failure Eldon Garnet

Walking through Clear Water in a Pool Painted Black Cookie
    Mueller

69 Ways to Play the Blues Jürg Laederach

Soft Subversions Félix Guattari

Speed and Politics Paul Virilio

Still Black, Still Strong Dhoruba Bin Wahad, Mumia Abu-Jamal & Assata Shakur

Why Different?: A Culture of Two Subjects Luce Irigaray

SEMIOTEXT(E) · ACTIVE AGENTS SERIES
Chris Kraus & Sylvère Lotringer, *Editors*

The Empire of Disorder Alain Joxe

جمع ابری باران نی اهدشد

نمی زد

جمع زمین سپید کوههاو

اگر دارو گان نوشته بند بشد

~~........~~

~~........~~

~~نسیم گل~~

نمم سکوت شب آن

آسمان

آرای درعان

دوست دارو دریا

دسته درت مال لا

سم ورسم او حبان

دارو گان

جمع جمله او اند

هبچ

٠٠